Larry Writer is the author of *The Australian Book of True Crime*; *The Australian Book of Heroism*; the Ned Kelly Award-winning *Razor*; *Bumper: The Life and Legend of Frank 'Bumper' Farrell*; *Pleasure and Pain* and *Never Before, Never Again*. He is a former editor, senior journalist and London bureau chief with Australian Consolidated Press and Time Inc. Magazines. Larry lives in Sydney with his family.

Also by Larry Writer from Pier 9

The Australian Book of True Crime
The Australian Book of Heroism
Sunshine and Shadow (with James and Stephen Dack)

THE AUSTRALIAN BOOK OF DISASTERS

LARRY WRITER

THE AUSTRALIAN BOOK OF DISASTERS

PIER 9

Published in Australia in 2011 by Pier 9, an imprint of Murdoch Books Pty Limited

Murdoch Books Australia
Pier 8/9
23 Hickson Road
Millers Point NSW 2000
Phone: +61 (0) 2 8220 2000
Fax: +61 (0) 2 8220 2558
www.murdochbooks.com.au

Murdoch Books UK Limited
Erico House, 6th Floor
93–99 Upper Richmond Road
Putney, London SW15 2TG
Phone: +44 (0) 20 8785 5995
Fax: +44 (0) 20 8785 5985
www.murdochbooks.co.uk

For corporate orders and custom publishing contact Noel Hammond,
National Business Development Manager

Publishing Director: Chris Rennie
Editor: Tricia Dearborn
Production: Renee Melbourne

National Library of Australia Cataloguing-in-Publication entry
Author: Writer, Larry
Title: The Australian book of disasters / Larry Writer
ISBN: 978-1-74196-902-3 (pbk.)
Series: The Australian book of ...
Subjects: Natural disasters—Australia
Dewey Number: 363.340994

Printed in Australia by Griffin Press, an Accredited ISO AS/NZS 14001:2004 Environmental Management System printer.

The paper this book is printed on is certified against the Forest Stewardship Council® standards. Griffin Press holds FSC chain of custody SGS-COC-005088. FSC promotes environmentally responsible, socially beneficial and economically viable management of the world's forests.

For all those who find themselves in the eye of the storm

CONTENTS

PREFACE

Australia is a land richly blessed. Yet it seems fate and the elements perversely balance our blessings by periodically inflicting disasters on this wide brown land. The word 'disaster' derives from the Greek 'dus' and 'aster' meaning 'bad star' and is defined as an event that causes major destruction and damage, loss of life and significant change to the built or natural environment. Bushfires, drought, floods, earthquakes, cyclones, epidemics, plane, train and vehicle crashes, shipwrecks and explosions have always been part of our history. And because these disasters – which are usually unpreventable – strike anywhere at any time, and impact terribly on the lives of everyday innocent people, they elicit from the nation deep grief and sorrow.

This book chronicles a number of natural and man-made disasters that have befallen Australia. It is not comprehensive – any attempt to make it so would result in a publication thousands of pages long. Rather, it focuses on a variety of disasters that have beset us over the past century or more in various parts of the nation. The very names by which they have come to be known evoke shudders in the national consciousness: the Queensland floods; Cyclone Tracy; the Granville train disaster; the Black Saturday bushfires; the wreck of the *Dunbar*; the Christmas Island asylum seeker tragedy; the Spanish Flu pandemic; the Newcastle earthquake. These are all recounted in this book, as well as lesser known, but – to those who suffered in them – equally dreadful calamities.

Though each disaster is inimitable, common threads run through every story: courage, sacrifice, kindness, faith in one's fellows. Disasters apply a blowtorch to the souls of those caught in their eye and the great majority of people, when put under unimaginable pressure, respond bravely, resourcefully and coolly. *The Australian Book of Disasters* bursts with heroes. Some people, of course – the looters and profiteers – react less admirably. Yet in the end, this book, while documenting calamitous events, is an attempt to celebrate the resilience of the human spirit in dire times, as well as the enduring ability of Australians to pick themselves up after being knocked down, and press on.

CHAPTER 1

THE WRECK OF THE *DUNBAR*

20 AUGUST 1857

Nearing midnight on 20 August 1857, while being buffeted by a tumultuous storm with gale-force winds, torrential rain and lightning strikes, the passenger ship *Dunbar* smashed into cliffs on Sydney's South Head. The ship sank, and 122 passengers and crew of its total complement of 123 perished: drowned, torn to pieces by razor-sharp rocks, or mauled by sharks. When it foundered, the *Dunbar* was in the final hours of an eighty-one-day voyage from Plymouth, England, and just 12 nautical miles from Circular Quay and safety.

The *Dunbar* was just north-east of Sydney Heads when it ran head-on into the storm, which was roaring up the coast from the south-east. Squalls and gale force winds whipped the waves into liquid mountains. The storm was so severe that the spray from the cliffs shot straight up into the air scores of metres higher than the towering cliff tops. The same front of bad weather flooded the Hawkesbury region.

Despite the terrible conditions, the *Dunbar*'s captain, James Green, a vastly experienced sailor and skipper, made the decision to enter the Heads, keeping the Macquarie Light on the *Dunbar*'s port bow. There was a terrified cry from a lookout: 'Breakers ahead!' Green was disorientated and came to believe his ship was making for North Head. He ordered the helmsman to swing the ship hard to port. It was a death sentence, as the *Dunbar* was flung broadside into the cliffs. The wooden vessel splintered, the mizzen and main masts fell, the lifeboats were staved in, and the vessel capsized onto its side as the monstrous waves crashed down upon it. One sailor, deckhand James Johnson, was thrown overboard and ended up on the rocks. He clambered up the cliff face to escape the pounding seas and passed out on a ledge halfway up the 50-metre cliff. Johnson was the sole survivor.

The *Dunbar* was a 1186-tonne, oak and teak, three-masted clipper. She was commissioned in 1854 and built by James Laing and Son at Sunderland, England. Construction took eighteen months and cost more than £30 000. It was the time of the great Australian gold rush, and the *Dunbar*'s mission was to transport gold-seeking passengers, and other travellers, between London and Sydney. But before sailing to Australia, she was press-ganged into service conveying British troops to the Crimean War. It wasn't until 1856 that she made her maiden voyage to the southern hemisphere. She was not just one of the world's biggest merchant ships, but – in common with the similarly doomed *Titanic,* which went down in 1912 – one of the fastest and most luxurious. The first-class section was always packed. On board on her fatal, second, voyage from England to Australia was more than £72 000 worth of livestock, machinery, furniture, cutlery and other expensive goods.

The disaster profoundly undermined the thriving colony's confidence. Journeying to England was a popular pastime, undertaken virtually without a qualm. The demise of the *Dunbar,* a state-of-the-art vessel with every modern convenience and safety device, emphasised in the most telling manner that Australia was an isolated and vulnerable country, and that sea travel was always fraught with danger. (This fact was further brought home to the reeling colony when nine weeks after the *Dunbar* sank, the timber barque *Catherine Adamson* was smashed to pieces at North Head, with the loss of twenty passengers.)

'A lot of [the passengers] were known to Sydneysiders,' wrote Kieran Hosty, marine archaeologist at the Australian National Maritime Museum. 'The *Dunbar* wasn't just another convict ship or immigrant ship bringing nameless people to Australia. It was a vessel which had taken wealthy Australians back to "the homeland". Those Australians were now returning to the colony on a vessel specifically built by Duncan Dunbar to cater for the Australian trade. It had very luxurious cabin accommodation, and it was very well crewed ... Imagine a fully laden jumbo jet crashing into Botany Bay today. The loss of the *Dunbar,* on the doorstep of Sydney, was catastrophic. It had a profound effect on the city.'

Yet that effect took time to take hold. It's unthinkable in these days of instantaneous worldwide communication, when we are apprised of events taking place on the other side of the world as they happen via TV, radio, computer and telephone, that few Sydneysiders – let alone anyone elsewhere in Australia or overseas – knew of the *Dunbar*'s sinking until late morning the following day, when wreckage began washing up on harbour beaches. It was days, even months, when all the inquiries had taken place, before the tragic and dramatic details of the loss of the *Dunbar* were fully known.

The first indication that there had been a maritime disaster came on the Friday morning when the captain of the *Europa,* which had docked in Sydney on Thursday at midday, reported that his ship had sailed in company with another large sailing vessel for five days, but that the ships had lost sight of each other in heavy seas and he had not seen her again. He did not know the name of the ship. Surely, he said, that ship should have reached home by now? Yet it hadn't.

Then, also on the Friday morning, the captain of the steamer *Grafton,* which had landed in Port Jackson, said that while entering the Heads he had seen floating in the water what he believed were the remnants and cargo of a ship: ship timbers, bedding, bales of goods, barrels of rum and boxes of fruit. In corroboration, word came of items that had washed ashore on harbour beaches, including clothing, bags and boxes, carpets, candles, silk, toys, drapery and bedding. Floating between the Heads were, among other debris, a handkerchief with the name 'Howell' sewn on it, the lid of a pickle case, a parchment label used for luggage on the English railways with the inscription 'Milne, passenger Edinburgh', a nightgown tagged 'Dobelle' and a cabin door with the brass number 68 attached. Surreally, a piano and a sofa also tumbled in the tides and currents.

That Friday, in the Legislative Assembly, Member Parker gave short shrift to the hotly circulating rumours of a shipwreck at South Head the night before. Although he had received reports of floating wreckage and of what appeared to be a topmast standing out of the water near the Heads, and people were saying they had seen bodies in the waters of the harbour, he did not consider such reports 'to be authentic information upon the subject and to detail mere rumours might be to agonise feelings for no purpose whatever'. However, he gave the assurance that the government was investigating.

As the day wore on, the rumours proved correct. Scores of bodies of women, children and men began washing ashore. Many of the bodies had been attacked by sharks. The floating naked body of a boy aged about four broke the hearts of those who saw it.

Some of the bodies were terribly mutilated. This, it was later explained by eyewitnesses, was because the shipwreck victims in the heavy seas off the Gap had been 'thrown by immense waves at a great height, and dashed pitilessly against the rugged cliffs, the returning water sweeping them from the agonised sight of the horrified spectators'. 'Here and there,' said another account, 'heads or limbs which had been torn off by repeated concussions against the rocks were thrown up as if in jeering mockery by the very element that had caused their destruction.'

Meanwhile, pilots Hydes and Robson, based at the Gap, noticed debris in the water and went to investigate. They searched south along the coast and saw the battered skeleton of a vessel. They had no way to identify her. They alerted police, who went to the spot, but were thwarted by the terrific seas.

Clearly, a ship had sunk, but which ship? Some said the wreck must have been that of a North American vessel that was due to lay anchor in the harbour around that time. Perhaps, mused others, it was a British ship, for a number were expected in the next week or so. Then a mail bag was dumped on the sand. On inspection it carried the name *Dunbar*. And hard on its heels came a cask of tripe emblazoned with the same word. A crate of cricket bats was, when recovered, found to have been stamped *Dunbar*. There was no doubt as to the identity of the lost ship. As the *Sydney Morning Herald* noted in its next edition, 'The hopes we entertained that the wreck would not be the *Dunbar* have proved fallacious.'

At Balmoral, a man saw the carcass of a cow floating in the water off a beach and began wading towards it to attempt to bring it to shore. He stopped in his tracks when, as he moved closer, he realised that the cow was being savaged by sharks.

A Mr P. Cohen of the Manly Beach Hotel saw two bodies floating and tried to recover them, but, it was reported in a journal of the calamity, *A Narrative of the Melancholy Wreck of the 'Dunbar'*, 'in consequence of the number of sharks, and the ferocity with which they fought for their prey, he was unable to do so'.

Some 13 000 people made for the harbour headlands, by horse, cart, omnibus and on foot, to see the wreck. Cargo floated in the water by the site, at South Head and in the harbour. Police were despatched to patrol the beaches for fear that the cargo would be looted. Bodies continued to be swept onto the beaches, and bobbed in the harbour. The recovered bodies – or what remained of them – were placed in wooden coffins which had been transported by horse-drawn cart to Watsons Bay, Mosman and Manly, and taken to the Dead House, or morgue, in the city.

James Johnson, still on the ledge he had scrambled to after being washed overboard, was spotted by a teenager named Antonio Wollier from the cliff top, and rescued. On the Saturday evening, after his wounds – remarkably, a few cuts and scratches only – were treated by a Dr West, he was interviewed by the Lord Mayor of Sydney, Alderman George Thornton, who reported to the colony in the press. His account is the most detailed extant of the demise of the *Dunbar*.

> I have been all day down at the scene of the wreck of the *Dunbar*, and had a long interview with Johnson, the man who was saved ... He stated that they were off Botany at half-past eight p.m., Thursday. The captain then stood off shore on the starboard tack, ship with double-reefed fore and main topsails; a very dirty, dark, and rainy night, two men were placed at the wheel. Captain Green instructed them to keep their luff; he had not been off the deck for two hours, since they first made the land some days previously. At about half-past 11 p.m. the captain gave orders to square away, which was done; the ship then ran under close-reefed fore and main topsails and foresail. As they neared the 'light' the captain ordered the foresail to be clewed up, sent the second mate to the forecastle to keep a lookout; then very dark; told him to 'keep a good lookout for the North Head'. The captain asked if he could see the Head. The mate replied no, it was solid darkness. The second mate suddenly called out 'Breakers ahead.' The captain ordered the helm to be put hard to starboard to bring the ship round, then blowing strong; ship on a dead lee shore. Having such small sail upon her, the ship would not come around (this was about 12 o'clock), and the sea lifting her in, she

> almost immediately struck. The passengers, who had all been in their berths, rushed up on deck in their night-dresses; their shrieks were dreadful. Johnson describes the scene at this time as the most terrible part of the whole. The ladies asked the captain, and entreated the seamen, to tell them if there was any hope. Almost immediately after, as if in angry answer to that expression, the decks burst up from the pressure of the water, the ship was rent into a thousand pieces, and all on board were hurried into the foaming and terrific sea.

Johnson told Lord Mayor Thornton that he and two Dutch seamen were among the last to be swept from the wreck. One Dutchman was dragged under the water and drowned. The other and Johnson, floating on a piece of wood, were swept onto the rocks. Johnson grabbed one and hung on; his companion was knocked off by a wave and disappeared. Johnson found his feet and clambered helter-skelter up the cliff. When he found refuge on a ledge high enough to be safe from the crashing breakers, he lost consciousness. The next day he saw the steamer *Grafton* enter the Heads. He waved frantically, but was not seen. He failed, too, to attract the attention of anyone on board the *Washington*, which entered the Heads soon after. He spent all day Friday and Friday night on his ledge. On Saturday morning, he waved his handkerchief and cried out to the spectators who had gathered on top of the cliffs. The sea mist obscured him from their view and the noise of the breaking waves made his screams inaudible. Then, purely by chance, he was seen by one spectator, a 17-year-old Icelander named Antonio Wollier, who bravely descended the cliff to Johnson's ledge and orchestrated his rescue by the people above.

In Thornton's account:

> The noble fellow … was then hauled up and received the hearty manifestations of the thousands there assembled. I opened a subscription, which was suggested by Captain Loring, of HMS *Iris*, and in a few minutes about £10 was collected and handed over to this courageous boy, who, in answer to my compliment

in handing him the money, said, in broken English, 'I did not go down for the money, but for the feelings of my heart.'

Continued Thornton:

> Captain Green must have taken the bluff north end of the Gap for North [H]ead for in ordering the helm to starboard he must have supposed that to be his position, and North Head a lee shore. Had the helm been put to port, the ship would have cleared, and run for the entrance to the Heads.

Thornton wrote that when he was at the Gap to meet Johnson, 'another brave fellow' volunteered to go down to the rock shelf at sea level to recover the mangled corpses that lay upon it.

> ... now a trunk of a female from the waist upwards – then the legs of a male, the body of an infant, the right arm, shoulder and head of a female, the bleached arm and extended hand, with the wash of the receding water, almost as 'twere in life, beckoning for help. Then a leg, a thigh, a human head would be hurled along, the sea dashing most furiously, as if in angry derision of our efforts to rescue its prey. One figure, a female, tightly clasping an infant to the breast, both locked in firm embrace in death, was for a moment seen; then the legs of some trunkless body would leap from the foaming cataract ... with feet seen plainly upward in the air ... to be again and again tossed up to the gaze of the sorrowing throng above.

Thornton and some others lowered the volunteer down to the water on a rope and he was able to retrieve a number of the body parts and corpses. However, as night fell the seas rose and a huge wave drenched the courageous fellow and those hanging on to the rope. They quickly pulled him to safety. Thornton returned to the city to write his account.

The inquest into the fatalities was held on 24 August at the Dead House. As the inspectors took their places in the hearing room, family and friends of the lost were moving among the coffins trying to identify their occupants. One of the first called was survivor James Johnson. The room was hushed as he described the moment of impact: 'Then we struck, and the screaming began ...' He went on to describe the passengers rushing about on the deck 'screaming for mercy' and Captain Green being 'cool and collected'. He told of seeing his shipmates and the passengers washed off the deck to their deaths, and of the masts falling. He denied that the crew had been drinking before the *Dunbar* collided with the cliff: 'We had a glass of grog at 12 o'clock [noon], but there had been no drinking aboard. The men were all very steady, good men.' He told of being hurled into the water with the Dutchmen and scaling the cliff.

Crewmen from the vessels who had sailed with the *Dunbar* gave evidence, along with a number of the rescue workers, doctors, nurses and police.

After some days' deliberation, the following verdict was delivered:

> The jury finds that the bodies viewed are those of some of the passengers and crew of the *Dunbar*, out of London, commanded by Captain Green, and bound to this port, and that the ship *Dunbar* was wrecked outside the Sydney Heads, close to the Gap, on the night of Thursday the 20th of August last, causing the death of the said parties: there may have been an error of judgment in the vessel being so close to the shore at night in such bad weather, but the jury do not attach any blame to Captain Green or his officers for the loss of the *Dunbar*. The jury consider it their duty to put on record their opinion that the pilot arrangements for this port are most inadequate and desire to draw the attention of the Government to the matter.

If the inquiry absolved Captain Green of blame, others, such as the editorial writer in the *Sydney Morning Herald*, certainly did not. The anonymous writer prepared the ground for his attack by praising Green to the heavens.

> No generous man will refuse a tear to the memory of Captain Green. In a profession which often calls forth the noblest

> characteristics – intrepidity, fortitude, self-reliance, and self-oblivion – he held a foremost rank ... He had seen much of ocean life; had a reputation as a bold, generous and successful sailor; had often cast anchor amidst the [con]gratulations of his nautical friends and the grateful acknowledgments of his passengers. He was a favourite in this port.

Then the editorialist violently changed tack.

> The memory of the late Captain of the *Dunbar* ... cannot ... escape the reproach of putting into obvious peril the invaluable interests at his disposal. Influenced, there is reason to believe, by a determination to anchor within a given hour, he ventured when prudence and the commonest nautical experience would have made retirement imperative. With the same wind and weather [other ships' captains] stood out to sea, whilst he madly approached a coast where a false manoeuvre or miscalculation would leave no chance of recovery or retreat ...
>
> Seldom does a vessel bring so many whose loss would be more deeply felt, or felt so long. Who with dry eyes can recall their fate? Many so estimable – many so young and so happy. What a map did time seem to open before them but a few hours ago! So cheerfully did they confide in the commander, that although within sight of the coast they retired to rest.
>
> That Captain Green died with those who perished through his mistake cannot be deemed an aggravation to his misfortune. Had he survived he would have been haunted with the distressing remembrances of sights and scenes which those who had no share in producing cannot look upon without horror ...
>
> We notice these facts with reluctance and sadness. Captain Green is beyond the reach of human reproach. Those who died with him had no time for complaint. In that agonising instant, other thoughts, we may suppose, occupied their minds. Could we imagine that every cry of anguish and despair fell on the ear of this

> unfortunate commander as an accusation, he paid a fearful penalty – far more bitter than the bitterness of death!

Just before 5 p.m. on Monday 24 August, the heartbreaking procession of the mutilated bodies of the *Dunbar* victims left the Dead House bound for the cemetery in O'Connell Town [today Newtown]. There were seven hearses, each pulled by magnificent horses. Each hearse was attended by mounted police. Following the hearses were four mourning coaches for the grieving loved ones, and after them came carriages for other mourners and dignitaries. In the procession was the band of the artillery companies, which played the 'Dead March' from *Saul*. The footpaths along the route, down George Street and then south along City Road and King Street, were lined by 20 000 Sydneysiders who stood silent and sombre, six deep in parts. Wrote one observer, 'Never can we recollect a scene in which the feelings of the people were so keenly and manifestly exhibited.' Church bells along the way sounded the death knell and all flags were at half-mast. Shops were closed, both as a mark of respect and so employees could join the throng.

The procession arrived at the cemetery just after 7 p.m., and there beneath a ghostly moon the last obsequies were performed by the Rev O.C. Kemp, his words echoed by the mourners. A few who died who had been identified were laid to rest in single graves. The vast majority, however, along with various recovered body parts, were buried together in a single grave. Observed the author of *A Narrative of the Melancholy Wreck of the 'Dunbar'*, 'It has been remarked that, although the time had not been specifically chosen for the ceremony, the calmness of a dim moonlight seemed not unsuited to the close of one of the most painful tragedies which has yet taken place in the annals of our colony.'

In fact, the funeral was not the close, because for days to come, more bodies rose to the surface of the harbour waters, and were processed at the Dead House and buried at O'Connell Town as hastily as decency allowed.

A subsequent inquiry into the *Dunbar* and *Catherine Adamson* calamities found that neither had been caused by the mistake of a captain; rather, each was the result of inadequate navigational aids at the harbour's entrance. As a result, the powerful Hornby Lighthouse that still stands sentinel on South Head was constructed in 1858.

Today, 100 metres off the forbidding cliffs at South Head and 9 metres under the surging sea, lies what remains of the *Dunbar*. The wooden hull has disintegrated over 154 years, and much that could be plundered has been, by salvors and treasure hunters. Happily, many items found their way into the Gillies artefact collection, which is owned and managed by the Australian National Maritime Museum and can be viewed today. But remaining there on the ocean bed are one Admiralty anchor and one Porter's iron anchor, piles of anchor chain, fragments of copper sheathing and ceramics, pig iron ballast blocks and metal fastenings.

In 2007, the site of the wreck of the *Dunbar* became the first shipwreck to be listed on the NSW State Heritage Register. When the *Dunbar* was destroyed, a Sydney poet, whose name has long been forgotten, composed a poem that was published in *A Narrative of the Melancholy Wreck of the 'Dunbar'*. It is as poignant today as it was when written:

> Warning not heard or seen – no help at hand –
> The wide dark bosom of the angry deep
> With irresistible and cruel force
> Received them all. One only cast alive,
> Fainting and breathless on the fatal rocks –
> To weeping friends and strangers afterwards
> Thus told his melancholy tale –

And of the lone survivor, James Johnson? Fittingly, he became a lighthouse keeper and with sublime irony in 1866, nine years after he himself was saved from shipwreck, he helped rescue the sole survivor of another wreck, PS *Cawarra*, near Newcastle.

CHAPTER 2

CYCLONE MAHINA'S TRAIL OF DESTRUCTION

4 MARCH 1899

In February 2011, the residents of far north Queensland battened down for the onslaught of Cyclone Yasi. Modern communications and meteorological equipment had ensured that people knew well in advance what to expect from Yasi. When it struck, they were prepared. There was enormous damage done, but not a person was killed. Things were very different when Cyclone Mahina roared out of the north-west Coral Sea and devastated far north Queensland's Bathurst Bay, north of Cooktown, and surrounds on the night of Saturday, 4 March 1899. Mahina and its resulting storm surge killed more than 400 people, still the largest death toll of any Australian natural disaster. The category 5 cyclone – as severe as cyclones get, and one of the most terrible ever experienced in the southern hemisphere – literally destroyed everything in its path, including the region's pearling industry. Its winds were recorded at 280 kilometres per hour with gusts reaching 360 kilometres per hour. The gale was accompanied by torrential rain and ferocious lightning and thunder.

The eye of the cyclone passed directly above the bays and beaches and giant granite boulders of Cape Melville, under whose lee most of the pearling fleet was cowering. There were other concentrations of vessels nearby. When the cyclone hit, the men of the pearling fleet were as unprepared for it as they could be. They were at rest after a busy week. The luggers had collected near their respective schooners and were renewing food stores, water and fuel, loading pearl shell onto the schooners and receiving orders from the skipper for the following week's pearling. Despite oppressive heat, a complete lack of wind and a 'black, leaden, fierce-looking' eastern horizon illuminated by flashes of lightning, the prevailing mood of the pearlers was described as one of 'joviality, rest and companionship'.

Because of the lack of communications in those days and the failure of the barometers to give adequate warning, Mahina took her victims by surprise at around 11 p.m. on 4 March and savaged all in her path in twelve hours of fury and mayhem. The great majority of those boats of the Thursday Island pearling fleet (six schooners and their sixty-six attendant luggers) that were not sunk at their moorings were picked up by Mahina as if they were toys and dashed to pieces on the shore or the Great Barrier Reef. Some 307 of the fleet's crew members died, as did a number of those who tried to save the shipwrecked men. For days, the bodies of the dead bobbed with the tides. Many were taken by sharks before they could be recovered.

In the wake of the cyclone, a storm surge, or tsunami, which was reported by some eyewitnesses as being 15 metres high, powered inland, engulfing and laying waste to settlements. It remains the largest Australian storm surge on record. When the water receded, tens of thousands of fish, including sharks, rays, porpoises, dolphins, dugongs and sea snakes, as well as dead birds and the carcasses of wallabies, were left stranded up to 5 kilometres inland. Reported Constable J.M. Kenny of the Eight Mile Police Station in Cooktown, 'When these animals and fish began to decay, the stench was pretty considerable.' Kenny added that the rain 'hit as hard as hail … The force of wind was so terrific that the trees had leaves, twigs, branches and bark stripped clean off.'

Mahina raged on south-west over Cape York Peninsula and across the Gulf of Carpentaria, took a half-hearted U-turn on 8 March and, as if exhausted by her efforts, petered out on 10 March.

A report of the cyclone, compiled by H.E. Whittingham of the Brisbane Bureau of Meteorology and portraying Mahina in all her fury, was published in the 1900 edition of *Pugh's Almanac and Directory*.

> This month will long be remembered, especially in the North, as the occasion of the most terrible calamity that has yet visited Queensland. On the 4th a hurricane some 30 miles wide swept the coast between Cape Melville and Cape Flattery, causing fearful loss of life and property. It lasted about 12 hours, and seems to have been accompanied by a tidal wave. It struck the pearl-shelling fleet in those waters with such terrific fury that six or seven schooners, over 60 luggers, and 25 diving boats were wrecked, and about 400 lives were lost. All but some 14 of these were coloured men, many of them single, but still they had those near and dear to them, and heartrending scenes occurred at Thursday Island when the sad

> news came to hand. The Government sent the steamers *Warrego* and *White Star* to search for castaways and assist the distressed, but very few living were found. Drowned were found in all directions ... Some idea of the terrific force of the wind and waves may be formed from the fact that trees were entirely stripped of leaves and bark, rocks [weighing tons] were hurled up on the beach, and masses of fish of all kinds ... were found hundreds of yards inland. A police camp on the Coen, about 40 ft above sea level, was swept away, the water rising to the waists of the men, and the wave rushed about three miles inland with overwhelming force. The lightship at Channel Rock, with all her occupants, also fell a victim to the wind and the waves. The value of the pearling fleet lost is estimated at £50 000.

The nation learned of the disaster in dribs and drabs. Scant bulletins began to filter from the tip of Queensland a few days after the cyclone. It was only when the steamer *Warrego*, which had been sent to investigate the reports, returned to Cooktown on 13 March that an idea of Mahina's impact was gleaned. Through an article headed 'The Queensland Hurricane – 14 White Men and 400 Coloured Men Drowned', published in newspapers throughout the land, the public learned that the schooners *Sagitta, Silvery Wave,* the *Meg Merrilees* and *Admiral* had been completely wrecked, with heavy loss of life, and *Crest of the Wave* had been dismasted. The names of the 'whites' drowned were published, and the article stated that 'the natives are burying the dead at Bathurst Bay, and there is a forest of sunken luggers' masts ... Thirteen porpoises were found 15 ft up the cliff at Flinders.'

Contemporary photographs of the disaster show the smashed luggers and schooners piled on the white sandy beaches in a mangled mass of timber. All around are flattened buildings and dismembered palm trees. People wander dazed and disconsolate through the carnage.

A Japanese sailor named Sugimoto left a graphic account, published in an 1899 publication, *The Pearling Disaster, 1899: A Memorial,* of miraculous good luck and of what it is to be onboard a doomed ship in a cyclone. He was a crewman on the schooner *Silvery Wave* and sick in his bunk in the forecastle when Mahina arrived. After a terrible night of being tossed on mountainous waves, he emerged onto the deck at dawn to see the masts broken, the bulwarks broken, and only a handful of fellow crewmen. The rest had been washed overboard. The area aft, where the captain and officers were quartered, had been smashed and carried off by the sea. 'Just then,' he continued, 'a big wave struck the vessel and I was washed overboard, but succeeded in getting onto a plank, with which I supported myself. Immediately I had been washed overboard I saw the schooner sink; the big sea had swept right over her and filled her up. I was blown and driven by the wind and sea hither and thither, and at last landed on the mainland at Bathurst Bay.'

Mrs Porter, the wife of Captain William Porter of the dismasted *Crest of the Wave*, would tell her harrowing tale, also published in *The Pearling Disaster*, of how she and her family narrowly escaped death when the cyclone battered Cape Melville, where their schooner was anchored.

> It is difficult to describe in words what a terribly anxious time we put in on board the *Crest of the Wave* on the night of the severe hurricane. I often think now of how thankful we should be to have been saved so miraculously ... At about 10 p.m. I began to feel uneasy and could not lie comfortably in my berth on account of the dreadful rolling of the schooner, so got up and put on a gown. My husband was out on deck then with all the men doing what they could to try to save the boats ... It began to sound very dreadful, and I to feel anxious. I stood beside the berth to save baby rolling out. By that time the water was coming into the cabin very quickly through every little opening, and soon the bed and we were very wet. While standing in my cabin trying to hold myself up and baby from falling, dreadful things seemed to be happening on deck ... My cabin got so full of water ... My poor little girl was frightened but did not cry much, she clung to me and hid her face under my arm. She and I both got sea sick as the storm grew worse, and it was almost more than I could do to help her while being ill myself. Things were washing against my feet and nearly carrying me away.

> The worst of all for us in the cabins was when the windows were washed in with one sweep, and the cabins filled with water. Baby was washed away from me, and I groped in the dark until I found her dripping wet and gasping for breath. My heart ached for her. I couldn't stand with her in my arms, and was just falling when my husband rushed in just in time to help us to the dining cabin, where we remained till morning, clinging to whatever would help us, the seas washing over us all the time. We had all given up hope long before daylight, as my husband told me we were sinking fast, and in great danger. All the boats had gone, and the sea and storm were too fierce to allow of anything struggling long in them. I tried to feel resigned, but couldn't, to the thought of my little one being tossed into that dreadful sea.

As if in answer to Mrs Porter's prayers, *Crest of the Wave* remained afloat until dawn, when the steamer *Duke of Norfolk* saw the wallowing schooner's distress signals and rescued those onboard. Captain Porter reported how he had encountered 'an Asiatic named Pitt, with two coloured women, who had all been in the water for 12 hours'. Pitt, who calculated that he and the women had swum 12 miles, had told Porter that he had seen the destruction of scores of luggers and many men perish.

Many people performed heroic deeds in the midst of Cyclone Mahina. The names of the vast majority were never recorded. One whose name has been preserved for posterity is Mohara, also known as Muara, an Erub Island teenager who saved the lives of her sisters, Mary Pitt and Louisa Oroki. John Douglas, the Government Resident at Thursday Island and a former Queensland premier, wrote in his annual report of 1899 that he had 'heard of many cases of heroism and endurance during the raging of the storm. One especially has been reported – that of Mohara, a girl of Darnley, who by her wonderful presence of mind and cheerful alacrity in the water was undoubtedly the means of saving two lives.' Douglas' request that Mohara's 'meritorious and heroic' conduct be recognised by the state led to a medal being struck and presented to her at the Erub Island courthouse on 17 November 1899.

Mohara died aged around 48 in 1929, and was buried on Thursday Island. In 2009, local historian Jim McJannett determined to learn more about the young heroine. He wrote of her in the *Torres News*, and, having read of her grave in the Thursday Island cemetery having 'one of the most beautiful tombstones in the north ... made entirely from (cemented) ground coral and pretty shells by the natives of Darnley Island', McJannett and his friend Omar Bin Awel made it their mission to find Mohara's final resting place. After a lengthy search, they found the grave beneath tangled foliage. The wonderful find was not spoiled for McJannett by the errors inscribed in the stone: Mohara's age was given wrong, and her year of death recorded as 1930 instead of 1929, but, as the redoubtable historian wrote, 'These things fail to matter. What does matter is the person, not only at the time of her heroism, but following. She was a good woman ...'

Another memorial, a white marble monument, stands in bush at the base of the granite headland at Cape Melville paying lonely tribute to those who perished in Australia's deadliest cyclone.

CHAPTER 3

THE SPANISH FLU PANDEMIC

1918–19

It was one of fate's cruellest acts. Just as World War I was winding down, the world was beset by a virulent and deadly two-year flu epidemic that claimed as many as fifty million lives – around three times more than died in the Great War – and in a single year killed more people than had died in four years of the Black Death (the bubonic plague) in 1347–51. Twenty per cent of the world's population was infected. Australia was not spared.

At the end of 1918, the last year of World War I and the first of the epidemic, the journal of the American Medical Association editorialised:

> The year 1918 has gone: a year momentous as the termination of the most cruel war in the annals of the human race; a year which marked the end, at least for a time, of man's destruction of man; unfortunately a year in which developed a most fatal infectious disease causing the death of hundreds of thousands of human beings. Medical science for four and one-half years devoted itself to putting men on the firing line and keeping them there. Now it must turn with its whole might to combating the greatest enemy of all – infectious disease.

It was early in 1918 when word of a flu epidemic in Europe, North and South America, India, Africa and Asia reached Australia. Tracing the epidemic's progress, it soon seemed inevitable to Australian authorities – particularly when victims started dying in New Zealand – that the flu was bound for Australia. Strict quarantine measures were imposed by federal and state governments at all Australian ports, and mass inoculations of citizens were embarked upon. Tragically, the precautions failed, and although Australia, because of its isolation, was one of the last countries to be hit by the pandemic, by the close of 1919 more than 12 000 Australians had died of influenza and hundreds of thousands had suffered attacks. Sydney, the most populous city, bore the brunt, with as high as 37 per cent of Sydneysiders diagnosed. Some 3500 in Sydney perished. More than half the Australians who died – some 6244 – lived in New South Wales. The world, and Australia, had never faced a flu epidemic so deadly, and have not since.

In spite of the soothing words of Commonwealth Director of Quarantine Dr J. Cumpston that the quarantine regulations put in place had provided Australia with 'absolute immunity' and that 'there is much evidence that the present epidemic form of influenza is the product of a slow evolution of an influenza already established in Australia [rather than due to] the introduction of fresh sources of infection from outside', the disease spread swiftly, breaking down the infected person's immune system and filling their lungs with their own bodily fluids, causing suffocation. Typically a victim would cough up a bloody froth. It was not uncommon for someone diagnosed in the morning to be dead by nightfall. There are reports of four perfectly healthy women playing bridge and by the following morning three had died of the flu. There was a children's rhyme whose jauntiness belied its dark message. Youngsters would chant:

> I had a little bird
> Its name was Enza
> I opened the window
> And in flew Enza.

While the influenza pandemic of 1919 was known as the Spanish flu, its genesis is thought by some experts to have been in China and by others the United States. It ranks as Australia's worst social and health disaster.

The conclusions of Dr W. Armstrong, Deputy Director-General of Public Health, proved more accurate than those of Cumpston and are generally today accepted as accurate:

> The theory which appears to best fit in with all the circumstances ... is that two separate infections reached Australia; one of low virulence in August, 1918, and the second of highly intensified virulence which actually reached Australia in January, 1919, and would have reached us in October, 1918, had it not been for the operation of the quarantine cordon.

The strain that caused the spate of more serious cases in January 1919 was introduced to Melbourne, Fremantle, Albany, Adelaide, Sydney and Darwin by carriers on a ship or ships docking from overseas. No vessel has ever been identified definitively as the ship that brought the flu to our shores. Victorian health experts immediately enforced measures such as unprecedentedly heavy maritime quarantining, the wearing of masks and an edict that Melburnians must not gather in public places.

The people of Sydney first realised the epidemic was among them when on 17 January 1919 it was broadcast that two flu sufferers at Sydney's North Head Quarantine Station had died, and a third had been diagnosed. All were from the steamer *Atua*. Then on 25 January it was reported that a soldier newly arrived from Melbourne, suspected of having 'highly infectious influenza', was being treated in Randwick Military Hospital. Two days later it was confirmed that two more sufferers, also from Melbourne, had been admitted. The following day, it was published in the press that a fourth person, again from Melbourne, had been laid low and was in Randwick Military Hospital, and that nearly twenty more were suspected of having the deadly flu. It transpired that many of these twenty – comprising soldiers and medical staff who were treating the stricken – had been infected in the hospital by the first victim. By 25 January, sixteen had died at the quarantine station. At that, the Director of Quarantine Dr Cumpston confidently, and against all the evidence, declared that the risk of an epidemic was minimal, and that he did not believe there was any need for popular alarm. He could not have been more wrong.

On 28 January, the *Sydney Morning Herald* published a lengthy editorial warning that Australia 'must now face the fact that the scourge which has taken so heavy a toll from the rest of the world has invaded her own frontiers' and, maybe unfairly, laid the blame squarely on the laxity of Victorian medical authorities.

> Perhaps our immunity was too much to hope for, but everyone will feel a most poignant sense of regret that after we have kept the epidemic away for so long it has at last discovered a loophole

> of entry. In Sydney we had it on our door for months, yet we succeeded in barring the way. We flattered ourselves that if the danger was not over at any rate the possible sources of infection were limited. The influenza, we thought, might be introduced not through the crowded south-east of Australia but through the empty north. We now learn that our precautions have been in vain, our vigilance stultified, and our hopes frustrated by Melbourne's failure to be sufficiently on her guard. The defects of state organisation elsewhere which omitted to make this form of influenza a notifiable disease and to take effective steps to prevent soldiers returning from the east from becoming potential centres of infection may perhaps lay Australia under a heavy burden. However this is no time for recriminations. We must recognise that the epidemic is among us and we must prepare ourselves to meet it.

By the beginning of February, twenty-three cases had been confirmed. On 3 February, the New South Wales government declared an emergency and ordered that everybody must wear a mask, gloves, goggles and body gowns in public to prevent contracting or spreading influenza. When people refused to be inconvenienced or appear, as they thought, ridiculous by donning a mask, and ventured into the streets without one, they were fined. Also prohibited were attending church, cinemas, theatres, music halls, schools, open-air meetings, libraries, pubs, restaurants, billiard rooms and sporting events. With cricket and football banned, returning servicemen were quarantined at the Sydney Cricket Ground and at the quarantine station at North Head. Today it is accepted that the restrictions had little effect on the spread of the disease.

Churchmen railed against the closing of places of worship. When asked to explain why God had not ended the terrible pandemic, one minister rather dubiously declared that the influenza had its genesis on the field of battle and the pandemic was clear evidence that God was punishing the warlike.

A government medical pamphlet, an influenza primer intended to educate the populace about the devastating illness, was issued to all:

> Influenza is an acute infectious disease that has been known for at least 745 years, although its precise cause was not discovered until 1892, when Pfeiffer of Breslau succeeded in isolating the infecting organism. The 'Spanish' influenza now raging ... is clinically identical with the influenza pandemic of 1889–90, which was known as 'Russian' influenza. In June 1893, a pandemic began in Turkistan and travelled in a westerly direction until all Europe was invaded. The disease is spread from person to person. There is no evidence to prove that it is spread by mail or goods. The onset of influenza is generally sudden, beginning with a chill or shivering fit. At the same time, the temperature rises, and may reach 105 degrees F. Headache and loin pains (which may be very severe) supervene, followed by general aching of the body and prostration. The most dangerous complication of influenza is pneumonia, the presence of which is revealed by high fever, flushed face, cough, increased frequency and difficulty of breathing, and sharp pains in the chest. As soon as one is attacked by the symptoms of influenza, bed should be sought and medical advice obtained. The best way of avoiding infection is to live a healthy life in every way. Live in the open air as much as possible, keep windows open at night and so secure free ventilation. Allow the sun's rays to enter all living, sleeping and working rooms freely. Avoid excesses of all kinds, including eating and drinking, and fatigue.

The Central Board of Health circulated a list of further precautions to take to lessen one's chances of contracting the illness. They ranged from plain good sense to the ludicrously useless. 'The public have their safety entirely in their own hands. They can prevent influenza's spread; loyal obedience to a few simple directions is requisite.' These included tying a white handkerchief to your left arm as 'a badge of safety and a constant reminder both to you and your neighbour at a time when in a sense every man is his brother's keeper'. People should also refrain from coming within a distance of '10 feet' of any other person, and from kissing, or coughing, sneezing or talking in another's face. 'Don't shake hands; instead, point to your badge of safety.'

There followed continuing diagnoses of influenza in every state and territory, except, for now, Tasmania, and with so many people seriously ill, virtually all commerce and trade ceased and numerous employees were put out of work. Consequently, the nation ground to a halt.

Few in the medical profession – which was already at full stretch treating the physical and emotional ailments of returning servicemen – were prepared to deal with the epidemic. And, at times, the dire situation was exacerbated by ignorance. In Newcastle, New South Wales, where nearly 500 would die and 2400 people contract the illness, the flu gained an early foothold at Newcastle Hospital when in March the Newcastle Harbour Master despatched an ill sailor to the hospital for treatment. Incredibly – because fear of the epidemic was by then sweeping the nation and the stricken sailor was exhibiting all the usual flu symptoms – he was diagnosed as having enteric fever and placed in a general ward. There he promptly infected the ward's sixty patients as well as doctors and nurses. It took an autopsy after the sailor died days later to confirm what the Newcastle medicos should have realised: that he had the dreaded influenza. The board of the hospital placed total blame for the misdiagnosis on medical superintendent Dr Norman Zions, who himself had contracted the flu, accusing him of having made 'a very great error which caused a great deal of pain, trouble and death'. (Dr Zions resigned his post in disgrace and travelled to England, where he changed his name to Dr Norman Haire, and became a world-renowned authority in obstetrics, gynaecology and sexology. Among many achievements, he was a co-founder of Britain's first medical birth control clinics.)

As the epidemic raged in the first eight months of 1919, supplies of vaccine dried up, which opened the way for purveyors of miracle cures to step into the breach and, in doing so, make a killing. The public was informed by large ads in the newspapers that such innocuous elixirs as Bonnington's Irish Moss and Pruno Antiseptic Throat Lozenges presented 'the best protection against the present scourge of Pneumonic Influenza'. The makers of Gumlypta Eucalyptus Oil and Extract, Inhalants and Joy

Baths exhorted folks to use their products to 'Kill the Germ Before It Kills Somebody.' Spruiked a dentist, Dr W.S. Peisley, of Newcastle:

> Will the INFLUENZA get you? Influenza is in the air! Everyone must be careful. Germs enter the system by way of the mouth. Keep the Gateway clean! Decayed, broken and loose teeth give lodgement to germs and become their breeding places. For your present protection ... have your mouth attended to now! It must be done eventually! Take the safe course and have it done at once!

And, brayed the pharmaceutical manufacturer Wawn's, if all else fails, apply Wawn's Wonder Balm up each nostril three or four times a day. 'Be prepared! See today that a packet is in the house (price 2/6) ready on the instant!' The snake oil proved even less effective than the government's compulsory masks.

One peculiarity of the influenza epidemic was that while no section of the Australian population was spared, it targeted healthy young men aged 18–40 over any other demographic. This was canvassed by Dr Kevin McCracken and Professor Peter Curson of Sydney's Macquarie University in their geographic and demographic probe of the epidemic in Sydney in a chapter in the book *The Spanish Influenza Pandemic of 1918–19: New Perspectives*. What McCracken and Curson called arguably the greatest disease outbreak in human history 'did not make an even sweep through the city. Males were more likely to die of the disease than females, people in their mid 20s to late 30s suffered the highest mortality, and some occupational groups were hit harder than others.' While, they wrote, no satisfactory explanations of this atypical patterning have ever been produced, 'The higher workforce participation of males (67.6 per cent) over females (22 per cent) was a likely key factor behind the substantially heavier mortality of men. Male-dominated practices such as drinking in hotel bars and attending crowded sporting events were other likely sources of increased risk of infection. But no definite connections can be proven.'

After the first deaths in January and February, the epidemic seemed to abate and the compulsory masks and other restrictions were lifted. Then it returned with a vengeance in April, May and June, with numerous fresh cases, many of which proved fatal. Again, Sydney was hardest hit. In April, the Sydney-based correspondent of Melbourne's *Argus* gave Melburnians a glimpse of what Sydneysiders were experiencing in the second wave of the epidemic.

> Sydney is drab this morning. Not only because of the weather, which is wet. The real reason is influenza ... we are disappointed at the virulent return of the plague. It was hoped that grasping our nettle firmly as we did in February last we had succeeded in reducing the thing to harmlessness. And now it is not only spread far and wide in country and suburbs and city, but also tenfold worse. The Government has reimposed the old restrictions, excepting that the hotels are no longer closed. Everybody is masked in trains and trams, and in the streets and shops. Black masks are on the increase. Yesterday Sydney stayed at home as the safest place. Worst of all, there is no Royal Easter Show, and probably no Easter races.

On the weekend of 28–29 June, sixty people died in Sydney and there were a further 276 fresh admissions to hospital. In Victoria in that period there were five deaths and sixty-nine new cases. In all New South Wales in the week ending 4 July, 677 died. On Friday, 1 July twenty-seven Victorians died. On that day in Perth, five died and a state record sixty-six diagnoses were made. In August, the first cases were recorded in Tasmania. These were among the last to occur. From that date on, the epidemic began to peter out and around late September, after which there were no further fatalities or diagnoses, it was deemed to have ended.

For Sydneysiders, it seemed the worst of the epidemic was well and truly over when the state government lifted its restrictions enforcing the wearing of masks and preventing people from gathering in public places, and allowed J.C. Williamson's to stage its pantomime 'Goody Two Shoes', a fairytale depicting the battle between good and evil and the triumph of love over hate, with many fantasy scenes and much joyous singing and dancing by the cast. The theatrical company proclaimed in its advertisements,

‘The people of Sydney have been wearing the tragic mask [to ward off the flu]; but tonight we shall enter the [theatre] wearing the comic mask. Incidentally, a new use has been found for that discarded mask. Held by the strings, it makes a perfect boot polisher.’

CHAPTER 4

THE MOUNT MULLIGAN MINE EXPLOSION

19 SEPTEMBER 1921

It's difficult to imagine, but the now-deserted town of Mount Mulligan, 170 kilometres inland from Cairns via Mareeba and Dimbulah, was once a thriving village populated by miners who worked the local coalmine, and their families. Today it is a bereft and windblown place, with the saddest of miasmas.

In 1920, in the Mount Mulligan coal mine's heyday, the mine was 'well-equipped and ... mechanically ventilated by a powerful, electrically-driven plant'. It employed between seventy and one hundred men.

Mount Mulligan, from all the evidence, was a happy town. It offered its inhabitants rough and ready – though perfectly comfortable – accommodation, a church, a hall, a school, two (well-frequented) pubs, a makeshift medical centre and a general store. It was a town where the residents worked hard Monday to Saturday and let their hair down after church on Sunday. Community spirit ran high among the battlers of Mount Mulligan, and rarely higher than the evening of Sunday, 18 September 1921, when a party was held in the town hall, with good food and beer, and singing and dancing to the strains of the local bush band. It can safely be assumed that most of the people of Mount Mulligan retired tired and happy to their shacks around 11 p.m., for tomorrow, Monday, was a working day, and the men needed a good night's rest before going back down into the mine dug into the mountain face which gave the town its name.

After the events of 19 September – events which were said to have made even the devil weep – no one ever danced or sang in Mount Mulligan again.

At 8 that Monday morning, seventy-five miners left their homes and, lugging their tools, walked the kilometre to the mine. They gathered at the pit head to collect their carbide lamps and explosives, then descended along a rope-way into pitch black passages to begin hewing the coal in the dry and dusty tunnels. The tunnels thrust into the mountain for 700 metres before branching into passages and tunnels, and the average temperature within them, summer and winter, was 32 degrees Celsius.

The mine was a disaster waiting to happen. Strewn on the ground were loose explosives, left from the previous week. The carbide lamps the men carried and wore on their helmets had a naked flame – potentially a lethal situation in a mine where there are flammable gases. But the management, Chilligoe Limited, and the miners themselves were sanguine about their use at Mount Mulligan because flammable gas had never once been detected in the mine; and, besides, they were so much brighter than safety lamps, in which wire gauze shielded the flame.

At 9.25 a.m. students at the Mount Mulligan school were gathered in the playground as headmaster Neil Smith led the daily morning prayers and the singing of 'God Save the Queen'. Suddenly from the schoolyard, Smith later related, could be seen what was described as 'an eruption of black dust' from the mine. Swirling high in the air amid the dust were timber and sheets of roofing iron. Then two seconds later came an explosion, followed by another, which could be heard in Kingsborough, 20 kilometres away. Smith, and the residents of Mount Mulligan, who had also seen and heard the eruptions, ran helter-skelter to the mine.

They ran in vain, for there was nothing anyone could do. Thick, black, acrid smoke was pouring from the mine opening. The two 2-tonne winding drums which powered the haulage system had been blown 20 metres from their frames. From the pile of earth, stone and timber now blocking the entrance it was obvious that there had been a massive cave-in. The outsized ventilating fan which circulated fresh air through the mine passages had been blasted from its concrete mount and lay, a twisted and smoking ruin, 40 metres away in a clump of trees. Every surface for 100 metres around was smothered in coaldust. Grass and brush was on fire. An initial rescue team which rushed into the mine to do what they could to rescue trapped or injured miners saw many corpses, and soon had to withdraw, suffering from carbon monoxide poisoning. After Tom Evans, underground manager of the mine, was hauled from rubble near the entrance terribly burned with a wooden stake embedded in his chest – he would perish from his wounds on 26 September – General Manager Watson sadly told the distraught throng, 'You'd better all go home. I hold out no hope for any man.'

The unconscious form of blacksmith George Morrison lay amid the debris. He had been working some metres from the pit head when the explosion sent him flying. When he regained consciousness – and for as long as he lived – he had no recollection of what had happened.

Frantic telegraphs were sent to Cairns and other regional centres for assistance from doctors, rescue teams and police. A typical account stated: 'Explosion throughout the whole of the mine, presumably caused by gas. The mine is wrecked, and there is much debris to clear before any entry can be effected. About 100 men in the mine are entombed and there is little hope of their recovery alive.'

First on the scene was a band of miners travelling on a pump railway car from the Tyrconnell gold mine at Kingsborough. Yet none could enter before a new ventilating fan – a makeshift machine made available by a butchery – was used to blow away the carbon monoxide that had choked the first party. Soon after came a train from Mareeba with doctors, nurses, ambulance officers and volunteer rescuers. They were joined throughout the day by other medicos and rescue workers desperate to drag free and treat any survivors. Sadly, there were none. The volunteers – with the exception of experienced miners who ventured into the mine to retrieve the bodies – busied themselves digging graves and doing surface work.

Of more use was the Cairns undertaker, H.M. Svendsen, who arrived on the train accompanied by a load of coffins.

It wasn't until nightfall of Tuesday, 20 September, with smoky fumes still wafting from the mine entrance, that the mine had been sufficiently cleared and shored up for large teams of rescue workers to venture inside the labyrinth of tunnels and workings that reached for kilometres under the mountain. On Friday, 23 September the seventy-fourth body was carried from the disaster site. (The corpse of George Turriff of Wonthaggi, Victoria, remained interred inside and would not be recovered until 10 February the following year.) This rescue work continued despite terrifying rumbling from the mine's bowels. Reported the official history of the calamity, written soon after the event:

> When each body was found, they were disinfected with phenol, carried from the mine on stretchers, placed in coffins and wheeled on skips down the ropeway to the goods shed beside the railway. There, each body was numbered and identified if possible. When

> the workmen were unable to identify a man, the wives of missing miners were brought from the surface to view the body.

For bodies mutilated beyond recognition, Indigenous washerwomen were asked to try to identify the corpses by their socks.

A reporter from the *Brisbane Courier* described the horrific scene when one body was borne from the mine.

> It was burnt black, and, with the exception of the boots, was destitute of clothing. The remains, which were scarcely recognisable, were identified as those of R. Thompson ...

In the same issue of the *Brisbane Courier*, it was reported that:

> Brave-hearted women, whose dead husbands and sons had been brought out of the mine, were trying to comfort each other, and urging those whose menfolk were among the entombed not to lose hope, as surely some of their loved ones would be found alive. All through the night and the day they stayed at the mouth of the pit, which is about a quarter of a mile from the township, making tea to refresh the men, and cheering them and urging them to greater efforts. Here, indeed, were true mothers of men ... wonderful women who, as their sisters have shown in the past, possess the British blood that makes heroines who can meet Death face to face and not flinch.

A Dr Clarke, who spent days examining the bodies, said he doubted if he would ever recover from the gruesome experience. He described the corpses as having the appearance of having been struck by a 'terrific heat flame' and noted too that every one had been damaged by falling timber and rocks. The skin of the dead had been carbonised and peeled off in flakes. 'All the hair was black and frizzled and a number of the men's heads had been crushed by falling stones.' One victim had been pushing a trolley laden with coal, which had overturned and fallen upon him. Another was upside-down, held fast by fallen timber. 'The most gruesome sight of all was several men whose position suggested that they had seen some awful object coming and had their hands raised to ward off the danger.' Dr Clarke observed that in most cases death would have been instantaneous, and one of the less burned men's lips were bright pink, which indicated the presence of carbon monoxide.

A patch of ground was hastily consecrated and a cemetery established. The victims were buried and their graves roughly marked. Suddenly Mount Mulligan was a town consisting largely of grieving women and infants.

Queensland, and Australia, were in mourning over what remains to this day that state's worst mining disaster. Queensland Premier Edward Theodore issued a statement:

> The coal mining industry is never totally immune from the risk of disasters. It is an industry that has taken a heavy toll of lives in all parts of the world, and in the face of the Mount Mulligan disaster, which brings the danger and uncertainty of it home to all of us, we can only give expression to a sense of the deep sorrow which the people of Queensland will feel, and join with them in conveying to the bereaved families of the unfortunate men who are entombed an expression of our sincerest sympathy.

Messages arrived from King George V, from Prime Minister William Hughes, from all the state premiers, and from the public. In every state and territory, people donated money to funds established to provide for the families of the lost miners.

A poet named Emily Bullock offered the following tribute to the dead:

> Women at the pit-head weeping, sister women stretch toward you
> Loving hands that hold for comfort your poor toil-worn hands in
> theirs.
> All our hearts are praying with you – may our love some strength
> provide you,
> May great spirit waves that reach you bring you healing unawares.

Ah! Today a wall of anguish smites us in the engine's shrieking.
And the grimy [red] dust flying seems with blood of victims red!
Still we vision those white watchers, tidings of the lost ones seeking.
Ah! Dear God! That for our comfort, heart's blood, life blood,
both are shed.

The theatrical organisation J.C. Williamson Ltd – as it had done before and would do in future times of great disaster – announced a gala matinee to raise funds for the families of the dead miners. 'All the artists, who are generously giving their services free, have arranged to present features of exceptional merit', reassured the promotional material. The show, to be staged at His Majesty's Theatre in Brisbane on 20 October, would include grand opera: the prison scene from *Faust* with Miss Stella Wilson as Marguerite, Mr Charles Mettam as Faust and Mr Tom Minogue as Mephistopheles; and the garden scene from *Il Trovatore*. The Gilbert and Sullivan Opera Company, under the baton of Mr Slapoffski and augmented by forty instruments, would present *Trial by Jury* (the jury being played by 'prominent Brisbane citizens'). For those whose tastes were more populist, there would be 'a melodramatic absurdity' entitled 'On and Off the Stage' and the burlesque sketch 'Fun in a Barber's Shop'. And the song 'Jazz Baby', currently 'the rage of America', would be sung and played for the first time in Australia. A guinea's worth of entertainment, patrons were informed, would cost only 7/6, 5/- or 2/6.

All up, the various funds to benefit the families of the victims of the Mount Mulligan mine disaster raised more than £33 000.

In the archives of the Queensland Department of Education is a letter from a Mount Mulligan boy, Herbert Smithson, whose father Bill perished in the disaster, to children in Mackay who had written to him and other fatherless children soon after the tragedy. 'Dear Schoolmates,' wrote young Herbert, 'We thank you for your kindness and for your letters of sympathy. Some day I hope to have the pleasure of meeting you. The accident happened at 25 past nine on Monday the 19th of September and they got all the men out, some on Monday, Tuesday, Wednesday, Thursday and Friday. The explosion started up at the fan and then in the tunnel. The blacksmith shop got blown to bits. The man who was in the shop got blown 200 yards away from the tunnel and after the explosion they went down the [mine] and worked all night and day looking for the men. Every day the people used to have breakfast, dinner and tea up at the mine.' Herbert Smithson grew up to become a coalminer, and in June 1942 was killed in an accident while working at Collinsvale State Mine.

On 22 September, the Queensland government announced that a Royal Commission into the disaster would take place, and on 2 December, after the three Commissioners had travelled to Mount Mulligan and inspected the mine, and taken evidence from Chilligoe employees, experts and rescuers, its findings were delivered. Most observers felt the cause would be revealed as the flame from a lamp igniting a pocket of flammable gas, but the Commission instead reported that the disaster was the result of 'the firing of an explosive, either accidentally, or otherwise, on the top of a large block of fallen machine-cut coal, such explosive not having been placed in a shot-hole. It is difficult to understand how explosives being used in the ordinary way could be fired in this spot. Alternatively, the conclusion that obtrudes itself is that a plaster shot was placed on this block of coal to break it, so as to facilitate handling, and it exploded prematurely, either because of a defect in the fuse or from some other cause, such as a fall of roof stone.'

The Commissioners believed that the ensuing explosion of coaldust travelled the working faces and passages of the mine, demolishing them and burning miners to death as it rushed on, and then burst from the entrance and into the air, carrying debris with it. It was this mass of coaldust that the children in the playground saw before they heard the ensuing explosions.

Then the Commissioners denounced the mine's operators. They blasted the practice of explosives being stored, used, distributed and carried carelessly and in disregard of standard rules. They said record book entries were haphazard and not according to regulations. They found that an uncertified deputy was employed at the mine. Inspections of the mine were conducted 'by men without colliery experience, without the necessary equipment, and were not made as frequently as necessary'.

The mine itself, continued the Commissioners, was 'dusty and extremely dry, and no adequate means were adopted to render dust innocuous, as required by regulations.' There was fine dust in the mine which, coupled with the dry air and the plentiful supply of oxygen, 'would be conducive to conditions which, according to authorities on coal dust explosions, were extremely dangerous'.

However, the Royal Commissioners praised the rescue efforts which were conducted without injury to the rescuers even though roof falls were frequent, ventilation was bad and many of the rescuers were inexperienced.

The explosion and the Royal Commission that investigated it led to the institution of sorely needed mining reforms. In future, mines inspectors would need to have practical mining experience, and their safety reports would be scrupulously accurate and properly filed. Only specifically designed and permitted explosives were allowed to be used in mines and the rules for doing so had to be observed to the letter. There would be no more naked lights; safety lamps would be compulsory. Well-equipped and ever-alert rescue stations would be established in all mining districts. Rules would be enforced for airflow and the use of ventilation fans.

The mine, in time, reopened and the state government ousted Chilligoe Ltd and ran the mine itself. Mining continued until abandoned in 1957. A shadow of tragedy had hung over Mount Mulligan since the disaster, and within weeks of the mine's closure the village was deserted, a ghost town. The cemetery fell into disrepair until in May 2008 a plaque was unveiled on the location by Indigenous and non-Indigenous former residents. It listed the 133 people who had been buried there, including the names of the seventy-five victims of the Mount Mulligan mine disaster. 'After the explosion there was nobody left,' said one who attended the ceremony. 'All the children were fatherless. Some of the graves have fathers and sons buried there. Some families lost all their men.'

Today, access to Mount Mulligan – should anyone be interested in visiting the benighted place – must be negotiated with the region's traditional owners.

CHAPTER 5

THE SINKING OF THE *GREYCLIFFE*

3 NOVEMBER 1927

It happened so fast. One minute the travellers on board the Sydney Harbour ferry *Greycliffe* – estimated at around 120 – were enjoying a glorious commute from Circular Quay up Sydney Harbour to the picturesque harbourside village of Watsons Bay on a sunny and windless spring afternoon; the next they were fighting for survival in the water, after the luxury passenger liner and mail ship RMS *Tahiti,* steaming at 12 knots, rammed the ferry and sent it to the bottom. The 3 November 1927 calamity claimed forty lives. Among the deceased were six children aged eleven to fifteen on their way home from school, three doctors, including the Chief Quarantine Officer of New South Wales, seven workers from Garden Island Dockyard, seven holiday-makers, Australia's first female pilot, an architect and a former mayor of Leichhardt.

The *Greycliffe,* a 38-metre long wooden double-ended vessel with a rudder, propeller and wheelhouse at each end, left the Quay at 4.15 p.m., steaming past, on its left, the construction site from which the south pylon of the new Harbour Bridge would rise. After collecting passengers from Garden Island ferry wharf, the vessel's upper deck and men's and women's segregated saloons were around half full. At the wheel was Captain William Barnes, 52, a ferry master with thirty years of experience on Sydney Harbour, replacing the regular ferry master George Gerdes, who was having a day off. As he cruised down the middle of the harbour with Taronga Zoo wharf on his left and Clarke Island on his right, Captain Barnes saw the ferry *Woollahra* chugging down the harbour from Nielsen Park and a tug towing a barge rounding Bradleys Head.

What Barnes did not see was the green-hulled, single red-funnelled RMS *Tahiti* – 140 metres in length and weighing around 7700 tonnes – approaching his ferry from behind. The *Tahiti,* piloted by the experienced master mariner Captain Thomas Carson, who stood alongside the skipper Captain Basil Aldwell on the bridge, had left Darling Harbour at 4 p.m. bound for Wellington, Papeete and San Francisco with around 250 passengers on board. An employee of the State Navigation Department since 1909, and having been before that a master at sea, Carson piloted around 250 ships a year and had never had an accident. (In what were later considered omens of the tragedy, as the *Tahiti*'s gangway was being lowered at No. 5 Wharf at Darling Harbour it crashed to the deck, narrowly missing a passenger, and as the liner was leaving, a girl who was farewelling it fell off the wharf and into the harbour.) Once the *Tahiti* arrived at the Heads, Aldwell would take over and Carson, a Scot in his late forties who lived with his family at Watsons Bay, would leave the ship.

At 4.45 p.m., the *Greycliffe* was just 100 metres off the *Tahiti*'s starboard bow. Suddenly the ferry veered to port. The *Tahiti* was too close to the *Greycliffe* and moving too fast to change direction or stop. Carson blasted the *Tahiti*'s warning horn. On board the *Greycliffe*, a horrified Captain Barnes and the ferry commuters now saw the bow of a ship three times the size of their own and fifty times as heavy bearing down at speed upon them. Carson swung the wheel to starboard. Too late – the *Tahiti* struck the ferry and rolled the *Greycliffe* over, and cleaved it in two.

The timber hull of the ferry was smashed to matchwood. The entire superstructure collapsed, sending timber and iron flying and causing death and injury to many on board. A number who had been flung from the ferry were killed and maimed by the *Tahiti*'s hull and propellers as it ploughed through. When the cold harbour water reached the sinking ferry's boiler, it imploded with a deafening roar and steam speared high into the air. Some parts of the ferry sank immediately, but others took longer. In the three minutes these sections of the ship remained on the surface, the people trapped inside the saloons and the upper deck struggled and clawed to escape. Those who could not went down with the ship, 85 metres to the harbour floor. Passengers floundered in the water, grasping the splintered wreckage for dear life. Many were sucked into the vortex to their deaths when the pieces of the ship sank to the seabed.

A Mr Corby from Moree told reporters how his wife and daughter perished in the disaster.

> We were in Sydney on a holiday and I thought we would take the ferry steamer to Watson's Bay and return to the city by tram. We were sitting together on the top deck of the boat viewing the foreshores of the harbour when I saw the dark bow of the *Tahiti*

> bearing down on us. People screamed from the other end of the boat and I knew something was wrong. I jumped up and rushed to where the life belts were kept. I pulled down the supporting lathes of wood and just as I attempted to grasp three belts the boats collided. I was sent flying into the air and while in mid-air I turned my head to see where my wife and child were.
>
> I saw that they had rushed panic-stricken for safety but their progress had been stopped by the mad rush of passengers from the lower deck, who sought safety above. The last thing I saw of them was the mother throwing her left hand in the air and holding my child tightly to her breast with her right hand. The boat then lurched to the side on which they were standing and then I knew no more.
>
> I was sent down what appeared to be fathoms into the Harbour and when I eventually reached the surface I searched among the struggling people with eager eyes for those who I valued most dearly, but I saw nothing of them. Not seeing them, I then did not care what happened to me, and everything seemed to be a blank, when I was picked up by a launch.

Police divers later verified that they had found mother and child wrapped in each other's arms under debris on the harbour bottom.

At the moment of impact, the *Greycliffe*'s engineer, Jack Barrett, was tending the engines. He heard a loud crash and was enveloped in smoke. Timber from the roof of the ferry crashed down upon him 'and sent me fathoms underwater. I kicked frantically for some time, trying to regain the surface, and just as I was going to throw in my lot … I saw a ray of light and came up close to a propeller'. Too exhausted to swim, and appalled by the sight of people drowning all around him, Barrett would have been completely content to slip back under the water to his death.

> Everything then was a blank. I rolled onto my face and could not right myself. I was swallowing water … it looked like the end. Then two small hands grabbed me, and pulling my face around, placed my hands on a piece of timber that was part of the wreckage.

> Although everything was a mist, I think it was a small boy. If it was, I am going to find him out and have him commended for his pluck.

Able Seaman Richards witnessed the collision from Garden Island. 'I noticed the *Tahiti* about 200 yards behind the *Greycliffe,* which had left Garden Island a short time previously,' he said. 'The *Tahiti* seemed to ride right on top of the *Greycliffe* and cut her in halves. The decks of the *Greycliffe* came tumbling down and I saw passengers flung in all directions.'

The collision flung *Greycliffe*'s pilot, Captain Barnes, into the water, where he was rescued by one of the flotilla of five ferries, launches and police craft which had rushed to the scene. After quick treatment of minor injuries, he returned to the carnage in a lifeboat to help others.

Rescuers plied among the floating bodies and debris, hauling survivors into their craft. One seaman from the *Tahiti* dived from the deck of the liner 60 metres into the water where he swam about in the wreckage holding the distressed and unconscious victims above water until help arrived. Although exhausted and in danger of drowning, he refused to leave the water, and had to be manhandled into a rescue craft.

Mrs K.N. Carruthers, who was a passenger on the ferry *Woollahra,* told reporters a harrowing tale.

> I was admiring what a beautiful sight the *Tahiti* presented as she steamed down the Harbour when I heard women and children screaming and then there was a dreadful explosion. Timber flew in every direction and the passengers of the ferry boat were sent to the left and the right. The *Tahiti* ploughed through the debris and struggling people ... The air was hideous with the screams of the drowning.
>
> I felt sick at the sight and was about to get in a place where I could see nothing further and then I saw my son Jimmy struggling for his life on a piece of timber. Almost immediately afterwards he sank and I lost all control of myself. I pleaded with everyone on deck to go to the rescue. Just as my heart was breaking to think I could not give any assistance – as, even if I had dived in I could

> never have reached him in time – he appeared above the surface. Women, crying frantically, grasped at the piece of timber that Jimmy was clinging to, and I thought that his fate was inevitable. He lost the timber in the whirlpool of human beings, but he managed to get another piece, and was clinging to it when a boat from our ferry steamer rescued him. He was on his way home from Sydney Grammar School and was in the company of six mates from the same school.

Alick Lawson of Watsons Bay was a passenger on the *Greycliffe*, and was sitting at the back of the upper deck when the collision took place. He was knocked unconscious by a piece of flying timber and came to in the water.

> I grabbed a life buoy and tried to get away from the mass of struggling people. Close by I saw a woman in a bad way, and I swam over to her and gave her my life buoy. I then got a piece of timber and kept myself up but I gave this to a man who was practically drowning. I then got a life belt and encircled it around my waist and tried to help as many of the drowning as I could. There were several terrible scenes, but the worst of all was a drowning man who had given his piece of timber to a lady and, being unable to swim, he sunk. He came up twice and on the third time, threw his hands in the air and went under, singing out, 'I'm done! I'm done!'

Able Seaman Richards and others from Garden Island boarded the boats *Bimbi*, *Sapphire* and *Waratah* and helped with the rescue.

> People were clinging to wreckage which was strewn everywhere. The water was strewn with ferry seats, ladies' handbags and pieces of the ferry steamer. Goodness knows how many of the passengers went to the bottom with her. The cries of the people were horrible to hear. I saw one little girl with her face smashed in. We dragged

> an old lady out of the water with her head badly injured and almost drowned. She was dead before we got to the wharf.

Survivors and the bodies of the dead were off-loaded at Circular Quay, the Man 'o War Steps in Farm Cove and the other harbour ferry wharves where, as the harbour air was rent by a cacophony of boat horns and whistles, gathered distraught loved ones wept and pushed their way through the barriers that had been erected to allow doctors room to treat the victims. That night at Sydney hospitals and morgues, people came to identify and claim their loved ones: husbands claiming wives, mothers and fathers claiming children, children claiming parents.

By nightfall, as many as thirteen bodies had been taken from the water. Next day Harbour Trust divers descended to the sunken wreckage searching for more bodies. They recovered nine, including that of a boy in a school uniform. 'I almost cried when I got his body,' said diver Harris. 'The little chap lay in my arms as if he were alive.' One man was found in a ferry seat, still wearing his spectacles and holding a newspaper. By Saturday night the death toll was twenty-nine, with eleven people unaccounted for. Over the following days, bodies floated to the surface as the sunken ferry that had been their tomb broke up.

The nation was stunned by the tragedy, by the loss of life, yes, but also the location of the disaster: the sublime waterway on a perfect spring day was no place for horror such as this. Flags on Sydney's buildings and on harbour craft flew at half-mast as a mark of mourning. New South Wales Premier Bavin rose in Parliament the day after and moved:

> That this House desires to express its profound sorrow at the loss of life which resulted from the serious ferry accident on the harbour yesterday, and its deep sympathy with the relatives of those who lost their lives and with those who suffered injury in the disaster … We have been so long accustomed to regard the traffic of Sydney Harbour as perfectly safe that this tragic happening has come upon us like a thunderclap.

Bavin then announced that he had been in contact with Prime Minister Bruce, who had authorised an official inquiry into the causes of the collision. A coronial inquiry would also be conducted. The *Greycliffe*'s pilot, Captain Barnes, was suspended from duty pending the inquiry.

Mass funerals of the *Greycliffe* victims were conducted at Rookwood and South Head cemeteries and as pioneer aviatrix Mrs M.M. Bryant, the first woman member of the New South Wales Aero Club, was laid to rest at Manly, five planes piloted by her comrades circled the cemetery. One dropped a wreath.

Meanwhile divers had the grisly and dangerous task of scouring the various sections of wreckage for bodies, an assignment made nearly impossible because the shifting tides were shunting the compartments all over the harbour bottom. On the Sunday, the 20-tonne ladies' saloon, which had come to rest not far from the men's, was nowhere to be found. It was found the following day, 13 metres away. On the Monday, salvage teams working with Harbour Trust cranes raised a section of the shattered hull to the surface and placed it on pontoons. There were three bodies within. The hull was examined by investigators. Pieces of debris washed up on harbour foreshores as far away as Manly.

St Andrew's Cathedral hosted the official Harbour Disaster Memorial Service on Sunday, 6 November. Conducting the service was Canon Cakebread. The mourners, including New South Wales Governor and Lady De Chair, heard the Canon end his sermon with the words:

> We love this city of ours, its wonderful surroundings, its happy people; but a sorrow like this makes us realise that in the midst of life we are in death. The death of these friends is a call to us to make the most of our life. We have met under the shadow of a great disaster and one so sudden that we can hardly realise it. This great city has been shocked to its depths. In a great city like ours there are constantly lives passing away, yet when some disaster happens all thoughts are focussed upon it. We see how near we are to disaster all the time. We realise how easily a great tragedy may happen. But we realise something else. While conscious of

> the uncertainty of human life, we are conscious of the courage of the human race.

When a Manly ferry cruised by the site of the accident on 8 November, its band played the hymn 'Lead Kindly Light' while its passengers, including a class of schoolchildren, stood to attention and doffed their hats. The divers and workers clinging to the salvaged ladies' saloon of the *Greycliffe* were visibly moved by the impromptu mark of respect. On 11 and 12 November, when salvage teams attempted, unsuccessfully, to raise the forward section of the hull, two bodies were released and floated to the surface, bobbing in the swell. It wasn't until 21 November that the wreckage was lifted clear of the water on huge slings attached to cranes mounted on pontoons.

On 12 November, five of the missing bodies were found floating in the harbour, taking the death toll to thirty-five. Two bodies were recovered on 13 November, and two more on 24 November. One body, that of Eugene Wolff, 59, an English visitor to Sydney, was wearing a jacket, in the pocket of which was £2000 worth of jewellery. His wife told police that they were due to return home on 5 November, and that Eugene had been to the city to reclaim the jewellery from a safety deposit box. He had kept it there for fear it would be stolen if he left it at the house where they were staying in Fitzwilliam Road, Vaucluse. It took nearly a day for divers to cut Wolff's corpse from the *Greycliffe*'s wreckage, where it was lodged between two heavy wooden beams.

On 8 January 1928, after witnesses from the *Tahiti*, *Greycliffe* and the public had been questioned at the Court of Marine Inquiry, Mr Justice Campbell delivered his judgment on how the disaster had occurred and who was responsible. Blame, said Justice Campbell, lay with the *Tahiti*, specifically the pilot of the *Tahiti*, Captain Carson. The cause of the collision was Carson's failure to observe the regulations binding vessels in Sydney Harbour, and that the speed of the *Tahiti* when approaching the point of collision – about 12 knots – was far in excess of that prescribed for craft navigating between Garden Island and Bradleys Head.

'From abreast of the northern end of Garden Island to where the collision occurred,' intoned Justice Campbell, 'the *Tahiti* was, in relation to the *Greycliffe*, an overtaking vessel' and it had been the responsibility of the *Tahiti* to 'keep out of the way of the *Greycliffe*'. He did not accept the claim of Captain Carson and other witnesses that the ferry had inexplicably swung sharply left into the *Tahiti*'s path.

Justice Campbell had accepted that Captain Barnes had not been aware of the *Tahiti* bearing down on the *Greycliffe* from astern, but those in control of the *Tahiti*, having the *Greycliffe* in full view, 'should have been aware of it but apparently were not, and a momentary inattention to the *Greycliffe* when the *Woollahra* was passing to port afforded just sufficient time to turn the potential danger into an imminent deadly peril, recognised by the pilot when he called out, "Good God!" and gave the order to starboard and sounded two blasts of the whistle.'

He continued:

> I am constrained to accept this view by the force of the evidence as well as by the consideration of probabilities. It seems to me more probable that the situation was allowed to develop dangerously in a momentary interval of distraction or inattention or failure of realisation, than that the situation of inevitable tragedy was created by an insensate act of an apparently sane man, that is, the master of the *Greycliffe* suddenly without any conceivable motive turning almost at right angles from his course and heading in a direction in which he could have had no desire to go.

Also, declared Justice Campbell, the speed of the *Tahiti*, at 12 knots – 4 or 5 knots faster than was allowed for such a vessel in the harbour – was a factor in the development of a dangerous situation as well as contributing to the destructive force of the collision.

> The speed of the *Tahiti* as it approached the collision was greatly in excess of the prescribed speed limit for outgoing deep-sea vessels navigating that portion of the Harbour. It must also have exceeded the speed of the *Greycliffe* which at the corresponding stage of his progress the master estimated [at] between 9 and 10 knots an hour.

In absolving the pilot of the *Greycliffe*, Captain Barnes, of any culpability, Justice Campbell accepted Barnes' claim that he had glanced astern when leaving Garden Island and had not seen the *Tahiti*.

> As at that time the *Tahiti* could only be approaching or abreast of Fort Denison, that is not impossible. It appears that he did not look astern again until just before the collision when, he says, the stern of the *Tahiti* was within a few feet of his port quarter and it was then too late to avert the disaster.

He did not quibble with Barnes' explanation of why he did not look astern in the interval between leaving Garden Island and the collision; that is, that he thought there was no need, as his speed was sufficient to keep him ahead of any outward-bound deep-sea vessel.

The inquiry's findings resulted in *Tahiti* pilot Captain Carson being suspended from duty. Living in Watsons Bay, the amiable Scot with the heretofore unblemished record was a neighbour of many of the lost. He became a pariah in the community.

The finding of the Coronial Inquiry into the disaster, which had been conducted concurrently with the Court of Marine Inquiry, was that both Captain Carson and Captain Barnes had been negligent, but not criminally so.

There followed a series of damages claims in the Admiralty Court against the Union Steamship Company, owner and operator of the *Tahiti*, from survivors and the relatives of the dead; and Union Steamship and Sydney Ferries Ltd made damages claims against each other. After four years the shipowners' litigation wound up and on 26 October 1931, Justice Halse Rogers found that 'both the *Tahiti* and the *Greycliffe* were blameworthy'. Contradicting the conclusions of the Court of Marine Inquiry, he ruled that, because the *Greycliffe*'s pilot had not looked behind him, or had been prevented from doing so by the faulty structure of the wheelhouse, and because the ferry did (as he believed) suddenly veer because of its faulty steering mechanism, the responsibility of the *Greycliffe* was two-thirds, and that of the *Tahiti* – which did not reduce speed nor sound her whistle when there was still time to avert the collision – was one-third. Both companies withdrew their claims and the case was deemed to have been disposed of.

The Royal Shipwreck Relief and Humane Society presented nine bravery awards to those who risked their lives to try to save others, and further awards were made in the ensuing years to four passengers, a *Greycliffe* and a *Tahiti* crewman, two water policemen, a police officer and a passenger from the ferry *Woollahra* who came to the drowning passengers' aid.

In his 2005 book, *Greycliffe: Stolen Lives*, author Steve Brew, a distant relative of the maligned *Tahiti* pilot Thomas Carson, insists that in being found at fault by Justice Campbell, Carson received rough justice at the Marine Inquiry. He records that a design fault in the *Greycliffe*'s wheelhouse prevented Captain Barnes from having a clear view of ships coming from behind, and that this was given scant attention at the inquiry. Also that Justice Campbell had pooh-poohed Captain Carson's claim that the ferry pulled suddenly into the liner's path, even though many witnesses swore they'd seen this happen, and Captain Barnes himself had testified that soon after leaving Garden Island he noticed a problem with the steering of the ferry that pulled the vessel to port, or left. Also, Justice Campbell had set too much store in the 'bow theory' propounded by Sydney Ferries Ltd, that stated that when a large and small craft are on parallel courses with the larger craft travelling faster, its bow wave could drag the other craft into its path, that theory having later been discounted.

The *Greycliffe*'s two engines were recovered and now reside in Auckland's Museum of Transport, Technology and Social History.

And today, beside the gates at St Peter's Church in Watsons Bay, where many of the *Greycliffe*'s passengers and their families worshipped, are plaques commemorating the memory of those who lost their lives in Sydney Harbour's worst maritime disaster.

CHAPTER 6

THE TASMANIAN FLOODS

3–13 APRIL 1929

The rain began to tumble down across Tasmania on Wednesday, 3 April 1929 … and it tumbled and kept tumbling. The north-east of the island state, in particular, and the Burnie/Ulverstone region, were deluged, the heaviest falls coming on the Thursday. In the worst-hit areas, the rain was torrential and ceaseless, and some 500 millimetres fell in three days. The Esk, Briseis and Tamar rivers, and others as well, swelled and burst their banks, and homes and drainage systems proved pathetically inadequate to cope with the deluge.

Farms and roads were soon underwater. Bridges were swept away by the raging torrent as if made of matchwood. Electricity and telephone lines were cut. Hobart was isolated from the rest of Tasmania when the main road and the railway line disappeared. After four days of incessant, heavy rain, twenty-two people had died.

Launceston began to resemble a vast lake when the North and South Esk rivers, which were running at 19 metres above normal levels, overflowed. When the city fathers realised that the town would soon be underwater, the post office bell was rung to warn locals to evacuate their homes and move to higher ground. The warning proved too late for some. Streets, houses and shops were suddenly metres underwater and many pedestrians were knocked off their feet by the rushing water and swept down the street.

Boats were the only means of transport and escape. As many as 3500 people were rescued by boat, and ferried, along with a few precious belongings, to safety at the Albert Hall and other centres. To make matters even more terrifying, there was no power. The gasworks and the hydro-electric power plant were rendered useless and the Duck Reach power station was simply carried away, leaving the town with no electricity for three days. The waters converged on the Tamar Valley from east and west, and the river rose to record levels. The mass of water that powered through Cataract Gorge on 5 April flooded more than 1000 houses near Launceston.

At Launceston, as elsewhere, members of the public as well as rescue workers, doctors, nurses and ambulance officers, Boy Scouts and Girl

Guides, the Red Cross and police offered their services and rose to the occasion, often risking their own lives. Brave men and women dived into the icy, swirling waters to help others. It fell to some to head out in boats and pluck people from the roofs of their homes. Some started clearing the mountains of debris from the streets, or took food, blankets and clothing to the stranded. Honorary constables were sworn in – many of them returned soldiers – and posted at houses and shops to deter, and if necessary arrest, the bands of looters that prowled in the town, seeking to profit from the misfortune of others.

Drivers of cars and carts flocked to Launceston on whatever roads were still navigable. Reported one witness:

> The motor drivers have spared neither themselves nor their cars in their endeavours, and the sight that was presented shortly after the sounding of the alarm when hundreds of cars were dashing to the scene was one that is never likely to be forgotten by those who witnessed it. There was no speed limit, and with headlights full on because there were no other lights, the cars tore through the city, and the air was full of the raucous notes of motor horns. It was truly a wonderful sight, and the manner in which the motorists dashed into the water with a total disregard for risk was a wonderful tribute to [them] ... If ever Launceston had reason to be proud of its citizens, it was during the past day or so. There were no social distinctions and everyone worked with a will.

One reporter recorded surreal scenes. Boats of every description were plying the flooded streets, while cars, vans and trucks were abandoned, up to their hoods in water. People carrying on their back what belongings they could salvage from their homes waded in waist-high water out of town to higher ground or the various refuge centres. It reminded the writer of a Venetian scene, 'though there was no glamour about it'. At the junction of Invermay Road and Foster Street a boy, not more than ten years old, emerged from a gateway.

> The water was nearly up to his armpits and he was struggling with a cat, which was attempting to get out of his arms. He tried to force his way through the water to a nearby motor lorry. He explained, 'I climbed onto the roof and got her.' However he had done so seemed a mystery for there appeared no one else at the stricken home. The feline instincts of the rescued cat were rather contrary, and no sooner had the boy placed her on the lorry than she dived back into the water. All efforts to persuade the little chap to stay were fruitless, and, eluding the grasp of those on the lorry, he sprang back into the stream and feverishly pursued his cat. The last that was seen of him was when he cornered the cat near a fence and took it into his arms once again.

One homeowner returned to his ruined home to find a dead horse in his lounge room. The animal had sought shelter in the abandoned home and, once inside, was unable to get out again. In a panic, the horse destroyed the furnishings of the room before drowning in the rising waters.

On the Thursday, the Cascade Dam on the Cascade River, 5 kilometres north of the tin mining town of Derby, burst. A 32-metre wall of water containing trees and boulders – including one 10-tonne specimen – careered down the Cascade Gorge and flooded the village, destroying houses, bridges and the railway station. The water also demolished Derby's Briseis tin mine. Fourteen people were drowned, including miners and five members of the Whiting family whose house was struck by the wave while they were eating dinner. The nearby Ringarooma River flowed uphill for six hours.

Word of the tragedy came first in a terse telegram from the Derby council clerk to A.L. Wardlaw, warden of the Ringarooma Municipality: 'Dam burst. Fourteen lives lost and families destitute. Will you wire instructions to grant relief necessary. All bridges down.' The missive did no justice to the horror. More apt was the description offered by a reporter who visited the town.

> Thrilling stories of the overwhelming disaster, occurring as it did with a warning of seconds only, were related by residents who told

> of the cataclysm which swept husbands to death in the sight of their wives, children from their mothers' arms and caused a mining disaster ... The heroism of the assistant manager of the Briseis mine, Mr W.A. Beamish, while trying to warn the miners to reach safety, the valour of senior constable W. Taylor who, single-handed in a small boat, braved the rushing waters and brought many men to dry land, and many other instances of supreme heroism serve to make what will go down in history as the 'Briseis Disaster' another bright page in the book of Tasmania's deeds of self-sacrifice and heroism associated with the mining industry.

Certainly self-sacrifice and heroism were not in short supply that Thursday; nor, of course, were horror and tragedy. Those who were there when the wall of water swamped the town of Derby and the Briseis mine would never forget it.

When the dam burst, the torrent swept down the river in what was described as a 'mighty turbulent roll'. Local man W. Kerrison stood awe-stricken as the wall of water descended on Derby.

> The wife and I were looking out of the window, overlooking the Briseis stables up towards the Cascade. We saw Richardson, Broadley, Bracey and Eadie coming from the timber stack towards the stables. Just after seeing the men my wife called out, 'The hill is slipping away.' I was standing at the back door. When I saw the water I called out, 'Run for your life, the dam has gone.' We ran up the hill about 20 yards and as I turned I saw the water rush in a huge, muddy foaming wave towards the stables. It took the stables in its course, together with several of the men and eight draught horses.

The wives of Broadley and Richardson saw their husbands drown.

Continued Kerrison:

> The water came within a few feet of our veranda and our house is about 70 or 80 ft above the level of the river. I thought I had nerve

> but I never want to see such an awful sight again. I saw the water rush across the flats to where the men were working on the lower face [of the tin mine]. It was impossible to warn the men. It all happened so quickly.

'My wife was standing on the veranda when she saw the water coming down in one high wave and swept Whiting's house away,' reported George Inverarity. 'She heard heart-rending screams.' The water smashed into the Inveraritys' house too. Mrs Inverarity was swept away, but managed to cling to a gum tree until rescued.

The baby of a Mrs McWatters was snatched from her arms by the water when their house was deluged. Her son William somehow grabbed the baby's leg and saved her. Tragically, another McWatters child, a teenage girl, was lost.

W.A. Beamish gave his life saving others. Instead of running for higher ground when he saw the water approaching the mine, he turned and returned to the face, crying for his workmates to run for their lives. Many did so, but Beamish was dragged under the wave and never resurfaced.

Also on Thursday, at Gawler just out of Ulverstone, a covered Ford truck with nine on board was washed off a bridge crossing the Gawler River and eight of the occupants drowned, including six of the seven Lynch children.

Not all the damage wrought by the rains and wind took place on the land. The ocean liner *Zealandia*, en route from Sydney with 190 passengers, was pounded by 15-metre waves and her wireless aerial was blown overboard by gale-force winds. So deeply did *Zealandia* roll and pitch that often her propeller was well clear of the water. The passengers were confined to their cabins and few escaped seasickness. One man sitting in a lounge chair in a smoking room was injured when his chair was hurled across the room by the motion of the violent sea.

The destruction wrought in the town of Longford was typical. Scores of houses were destroyed and 200 people were left homeless. At midday on Friday, 5 April, the town seemed likely to avoid being flooded despite the teeming rain. By 1.30 a.m., the town was swamped by a metre of water. People with two-storey houses scampered to the top floor; those with only a single storey were forced to abandon their homes. There were numerous rescues by boats, and craft were tethered to trees in the streets. As day dawned on Monday, 8 April, the water had subsided, but left in its wake half a metre of thick, viscous mud and slime and debris. Affleck's Mill, which had stood in the town longer than almost any other building, was so badly inundated it had to be demolished.

Because of the large numbers of drowned domestic and farm animals, outbreaks of disease were feared. E.J. Tudor, Tasmania's Secretary for Public Health, issued a health warning to the public:

> In view of the possibility of outbreaks of infectious disease following the floods in the northern part of the state, the Public Health Department is taking active measures to cope with the position as far as is possible. The South Esk River, which is the source of water supply in five large towns, has been polluted by the carcasses of dead animals and other offensive matter and the local authorities concerned have been instructed to warn all residents to boil all water required for domestic purposes as a safeguard against the outbreak of disease. As soon as the flood waters have subsided, officers of the department will make a survey of the river with the object of ascertaining the extent of pollution and will also advise means and assist local authorities as far as practicable to place the supply in a satisfactory state.

Tudor added that he was despatching Chief Inspector Riley with 'disinfecting apparatus' to cleanse premises before they were occupied again. Fumigating inspectors were also assigned to test meat being sold for human consumption to ensure it had not come from contaminated carcasses.

Thousands of pounds were raised, from within Tasmania and the rest of Australia, and Great Britain, and allocated to the areas most in need. J.C. Williamson's, the theatrical producers, staged performances of *The Student Prince* in Hobart and Launceston. The actors and behind-the-scenes crews worked for nothing and the takings were channelled into the relief fund. Because of the enormous demand, seats at the shows were auctioned, which led to more money being raised. There were also public pleas for clothing, footwear, blankets and food, and these were generously met.

Looting was not confined to Launceston. Many people caught stealing from abandoned homes were arrested by police, or dealt with by furious townspeople.

Because Hobart was out of contact with the rest of the state, news of the havoc caused by the rain and flooding came in gradually over the first few days. It was only on the Saturday that people in the capital had any idea of the enormous toll taken on Tasmania. An aghast editorialist in Hobart's *Mercury* said that while Hobart was 'isolated from the sources of knowledge by the total failure of the means of communication … there has been disaster after disaster in widely different places, accompanied by an almost general devastation … As a rule we escape in this well-situated island the ravages of hurricanes, typhoons, tropical thunderstorms, earthquakes, volcanic outbursts, tidal waves, water spouts and other throes and visitations to which tropical and less-favoured countries are subject. Yet we have our strong sun, high winds and water deluges occasionally to test and sometimes to destroy the puny handiworks of man.'

The writer then reeled off the known rollcall of calamity:

> … the disastrous floods in the north, centre and east of the state; the washing away of substantially-built bridges and flimsier structures; the bursting of the great dam at the Briseis mine; a landslide on the northern coastal railway; the loss of lives; the havoc amongst orchards and properties and the general swamping, blocking and destruction of roads and railways …

By 12 April, the sun was shining again and the flood waters had receded. The great mop-up commenced. Debris and silt were removed from streets and houses by emergency workers and gangs of volunteers. Water-spoiled goods were dumped and burned. While vast numbers were homeless and living in camps, some people were able to gingerly return to their homes and begin to clean and disinfect the premises. Railway lines and postal, telephone and telegraph services were restored. Bridges were rebuilt. The proceeds of relief funds were distributed to the needy.

Yet, while spirits were lifting, each day brought terrible reminders of the great flood of 1929, and no reminder was more heart-rending than the discovery of the final two unaccounted-for bodies of those killed in the Briseis mine. The remains of Jack Brodie and Hector McCormack were disinterred from the mud, some 6 kilometres from the mine. McCormack left behind a widow and two children.

CHAPTER 7

THE GREAT MELBOURNE STORM

30 NOVEMBER–3 DECEMBER 1934

Today, Melbourne hosts a successful rugby league team, the Melbourne Storm. The team is more aptly named than its band of devoted supporters realise.

On Thursday, 28 November 1934, two days before the great storm, Melbourne was engulfed by an eerie stillness. The weather was hot and muggy, and the winds that had recently buffeted southern Victoria had petered out. Many Melburnians, still elated after the city's recent centenary celebrations and looking forward to Christmas, later claimed that in the days leading up to the storm, feelings of well-being were inexplicably supplanted by waves of anxiety, a sense of dread that something terrible was about to befall them. Whether real or hindsight imaginings, something terrible did befall the city and surrounds day and night, non-stop, from 30 November to 3 December.

It had been a wet spring, with an unusual number of storms and much bucketing rain; then, on 29 November, a cold front swept across the state. In its wake, barometers plummeted as a depression developed in Bass Strait and formed a cyclonic centre. Torrential rain began to fall in central Victoria and Gippsland, and grew heavier, descending from the leaden sky in metallic sheets. In Melbourne, 140 millimetres of rain fell in the forty-eight hours ending on 1 December, and rainfall was even more intense in this period east of Melbourne and over South Gippsland, with over 350 millimetres falling. Roads were submerged, houses were inundated and evacuated, bridges and tram and railway lines washed out and vehicles swept from thoroughfares. The Yarra and other rivers and creeks burst their banks, isolating towns and flooding the countryside. Flooding unprecedented in living memory was widespread over the Yarra Valley, the Latrobe River district and South Gippsland, with enormous loss of livestock, property and crops. When Moonee Ponds Creek broke, water was 1.5 metres deep in the streets of Kensington. Dams burst at Emerald, and according to the *Argus,* 60 000 tons of water coursed through the breach.

A south-west wind strengthened throughout Thursday night and blew mightily over the affected area, soon reaching gale force. Trees and buildings were flattened or damaged by the violent 140-kilometre per hour squalls and blasts. At sea, the winds whipped up enormous waves that caused the steamer *Triona* to run aground on South Melbourne beach, and sank yachts and fishing and leisure craft. Passenger liners were helpless in the furious seas, and tugs were unable to go to their rescue for fear of sinking.

Over the next four days, if people had not been so preoccupied saving themselves and their property they would have been appalled by the despatches about the terrible damage inflicted by the tempest. By the time the storm and consequent flooding ended, thirty-five had perished, eighteen by drowning, and 6000 were left homeless.

At Eltham, elderly William Frizell and his wife were snatched by rescuers in a boat from the roof of their all-but-submerged home minutes before it disappeared underwater. Down the road, a man who refused an order to abandon his car was nearly drowned. He clambered from his vehicle at the last moment and tried to reach safety by climbing along telegraph wires, but fell into the raging waters. A number of local volunteers linked hands and the rescuer at the end of the human chain managed to grasp the man as he was about to be swept to his death in the lagoon.

At Montague, Alfred Davies, John Greenberry and Leonard Crook were electrocuted when they came into contact with a pool of water that had been electrified by a fallen wire. The horse Crook had been riding stepped on the wire and was killed. Crook was thrown into the electrified water and also died instantly. Davies and Greenberry, thinking Crook had been knocked unconscious by the fall, ran to his aid, stepping into the death trap pool and perishing themselves. And at St Kilda, George Somerville died when, while watching the huge seas, he trod on an exposed electrical wire that was lying on the ground after its pole had been knocked down by the wind.

Douglas Garland, a caretaker at the Dunlop factory at Collingwood, suffered a fatal heart attack while desperately trying to carry manufacturing equipment out of the rising waters.

Also at St Kilda, wrestler George Foskett was watching the roiling seas crashing on the pier when he saw two young men who had ventured out towards the end of the jetty knocked down and into the water by a wave. One clambered to safety, but there was no sign of the other. 'I ran along the pier,' said Foskett, 'and waves knocked me over at least half a dozen times. When I reached the man, he said, "He's gone. He's gone." Clinging together, we made our way back along the pier.'

J. Lamb, caretaker of the Middle Bay baths, told a harrowing tale. From midnight on 29 November, he, his mother and his three younger sisters were bunkered down, fully dressed and scared for their lives, in their house near the baths, listening to the terrific roar of the pounding sea. On the Friday, the club rooms at the baths were demolished by the waves.

> I tried to save a wireless set and other valuable gear in the rooms, but the force of the wind and waves prevented me. As the wind increased, dressing rooms crumpled up one by one, and beams were caught on the waves, carried forward like match wood and dashed against the house. I was afraid that our house would collapse so we evacuated.

Meanwhile, the proprietor of bayside Mentone baths was experiencing similar terror. 'The whole of the floor of my house is heaving beneath my feet,' reported A.J. Callway. 'Waves are bursting through the floor and the building is shaking. Most of the walls of the baths have been washed away or severely damaged … I have never known such seas in the bay.'

Mentone residents who tried to take refuge – and their minds off the storm – in the local picture house were thwarted when water inundated the theatre, quickly rising to a metre in depth. The projectionist abandoned his post, the projector clattered to a stop and the patrons ran for the relative shelter of their homes.

The City of Mentone lost its gas supply, as well as its electricity, when the gasworks was inundated, and three million bees drowned when floodwaters swamped and overturned hives at an apiary at Tooroonga.

The proprietors of Wirth's Circus – which had prided itself on ensuring that the show went on despite fire and flood in the past – had no qualms about cancelling its Gippsland tour.

Near Moe, farmer David Beck and his family fled from their submerged home and sheltered for two days and nights in the sty with their pigs. When they were finally able to inspect the damage to their property they found eighteen cows and calves drowned in their washhouse, and six other carcasses in their house. Another cow had climbed into Beck's truck and perished grotesquely with its front legs sticking through the steering wheel.

The *Argus* reported that:

> In Meredith Street, [in seaside] Elwood, the flood was most severe. Huge breakers washed over the stone retaining wall and sent the water rushing up the roadway for more than 200 yards. Even 100 yards from the beach the water was 5ft deep, and most of the residents for that distance had to vacate their homes. Mr and Mrs M. Brannigan were the first to go. Before 5 p.m. several inches of water covered the floors and after pulling up the carpet and stacking the furniture, Mr Brannigan and his family donned bathing suits and overcoats and waded through the quickly rising flood to a friend's car, which could not approach closer than 150 metres. Mr and Mrs Hubbard quickly followed the Brannigans, and by 6.30 p.m. most of the houses in the streets near the beach were deserted. By 8 p.m. several feet of water covered the floors of these houses.

Four Chinese gardeners were forced by the rising waters onto the roof of a house at Heidelberg at around 5 p.m. When the waters continued to rise, and the house became submerged, they managed to reach a nearby tree. A small rowing boat was sent to rescue the men, but could only take two of them. The strength of the current prevented the rescuers from returning, and the other two men were forced to wait in the tree until 10.30 a.m. the next day, when police came to get them in a motorboat.

Six people drowned and as many as 2000 were made homeless when the little farming town of Koo Wee Rup and about 50 square kilometres of surrounding farms and farmland were inundated by floodwaters that coursed down from the hills to the north. The water rose by 30 centimetres every minute and soon reached a depth of over 2 metres in the streets. Many locals spent the night on their rooftops, and there they faced the extra terror of having to fight off with sticks – or whatever else was handy – hundreds of swimming snakes that slithered onto the roofs. Next day, the residents were rescued by boats and piled into trains that had been despatched from Melbourne.

Incredibly, Mary Ann Bolleman, a patient in Koo Wee Rup Hospital, held a baby above her head for fifteen hours as the waters surged around her, before they were both rescued.

Other stories did not have so happy an outcome. At Garfield, the body of the elderly George Wilson was found dead in his bed in his hut. He had drowned while asleep. Schoolboy Kevin Sims, aged 6, was caught in the rising waters and drowned in Gilfedders Creek, near Mirboo North. The creek had broken its banks for the first time in its history. His father went to search for his missing son, and he was horrified to find Gilfedders Creek had become a waterway 150 metres wide. When the water finally receded, Kevin's body was found in the branches of a tree.

The Latrobe River rose 3 metres over the Princes Highway at Rosedale. At Loy Yang, which found itself in the middle of a lake 2 kilometres wide, thousands of sheep and cattle drowned. Many distraught farmers who had refused to abandon their farms had to be plucked from rooftops at the last minute.

Among many who acted heroically, one A. Briggs distinguished himself by making many trips swimming beside his horse from house to house, carrying to safety men, women and children who had been trapped on their roofs.

In the Melbourne central business district, all was chaos. Rainwater gushed down the streets and footpaths, knocking pedestrians down. Signs and awnings were blown loose by the wind and sent hurtling through the air. Many people were hurt, and some hospitalised. Offices and shops emptied of customers and staff as commuters rushed to their homes in the suburbs to be with their families. Trams and trains were brought to a standstill by the teeming rain and wild winds. Cars stalled and were left in the street. Some 120 millimetres of rain fell in the city in the twenty-four hours from midnight on Thursday, 29 November. The wind tore through the concrete and timber canyons at 110 kilometres per hour.

Every suburb of Melbourne suffered damage. Thousands of trees, many of them substantial and long-established, were uprooted, bringing power lines down with them. Branches were torn off and flung into the air and gardens were destroyed. Windows and roofs were broken and battered. Gutters overflowed and flooded the streets. Parks resembled swimming pools. The Fitzroy Gardens lost a number of its prized full-grown poplar trees and its glorious gardens – which had been tended for months in preparation for the recent centenary celebrations – were washed away. Bunting and flags which had been erected in the city and suburbs for the big centenary party were torn free and blown away. Melbourne Town Clerk McCall cancelled all leave for parks and gardens employees and ordered them to be on call and ready to leap into action if needed.

Lord Mayor Wales pleaded with all Australians to pitch in and donate money to a fund established to help ease the suffering, saying:

> Victoria has been visited by one of the worst calamities in her history. Several people have lost their lives, many have been rendered homeless and others have lost all or most of their possessions. The position of many of these unfortunate people is desperate and action must be taken immediately to afford them relief. The situation calls for sacrifice.

Added Premier Sir Stanley Argyle, exhorting constituents to dig deep, 'We have just celebrated the completion of 100 years of wonderful progress. Let us face the present situation in the same spirit of determination that made Victoria a state of which we are so proud.'

Suburban schools, churches, sports clubs and community centres were opened to accommodate those whose homes had been made uninhabitable.

On Saturday, 1 December, wreckage from the coastal steamer *Coramba*, and the bodies of the *Coramba*'s second mate, R.M. Wishart, and a seaman, T. Byrne, were found washed ashore on the southern coast of Phillip Island. No hope was held for the vessel, which left Warrnambool on 29 November, or its missing crew of seventeen. The sea and air search that recovered the debris and the bodies was instigated when the *Coramba,* which did not carry wireless, did not dock at Melbourne on schedule on 30 November.

Other ships were missing, too, and the large passenger liner *Jervis Bay,* with about 300 passengers on board – including Boy Scouts from India and the United Kingdom who had come for the international jamboree – could not dock, so was forced to remain at anchor, being pummelled by the heavy seas.

On Monday, 3 December, as the storm eased a little and the floodwaters began to fall, the *Argus* updated readers on the disaster.

> Many people have died and thousands are homeless after homes have been submerged as a result of the greatest flood in the history of the Yarra. From Warburton to Melbourne, the Yarra has become a series of vast lakes connected by swirling rapids. Much splendid rescue work has been performed. Officials of the weather bureau said last night that the present flood appeared to be a record one ...
>
> Nature, in one of her most destructive moods, has spread havoc over large portions of the Melbourne metropolitan area and Gippsland. Fed by heavy and incessant rains over the watersheds, the Yarra and lesser streams have become turbid and fast-flowing wastes of waters, breaking their bounds and inundating large areas of the surrounding country. In some places, whole settlements have been invaded by the flood waters, dwellings have been ruined, stock and property have been swept away, bridges have been demolished, railway and road services have been interrupted. Worst of all, numerous lives have been lost, including those of the officers and crew of the small steamer *Coramba* ...
>
> The whole community has been shocked by the magnitude of the disaster in both its human and economic aspects. The one heartening fact among the general sadness is the readiness with which those who have escaped the ravages of the floods are

> expressing sympathy with the victims. This characteristic response of a warm-hearted people to the appeal made by the misfortunes of their fellow-beings is already finding tangible expression in generous contributions to the relief funds which have been promptly organised.

The next day, a third body from the *Coramba*, that of chief officer D. Sinclair, was discovered wedged between rocks and encased in kelp near Pyramid Rock on Phillip Island. Nearby was more wreckage from the *Coramba*, including a gangway, life jackets, portions of the deckhouse, a varnished spar, wooden deck fittings and a tin of ship's biscuits. In the days that followed the *Coramba*'s disappearance a salvage diver was commissioned to find the hull. He reported back that the sunken ship was lying in pieces in roughly 50 metres of water, about 2.5 kilometres west of Seal Rocks, on the far south-western tip of Phillip Island. Attempts to relocate the vessel were made, but failed, and today, seventy-seven years later, it remains lost.

By midweek, as the rain and wind stopped, mopping up began. Gifts of money, food, clothes, blankets and livestock were distributed to the victims. People opened their homes to the homeless. The Victorian government made it clear it would not be providing funds to repair private property damaged by the storms and the floods – that would be the responsibility of owners, local councils, insurance companies and charity funds. But it earmarked an initial £150 000 – with more to come as required – to reconstruct foreshores, jetties and piers, bridges, roads and tram and train tracks, strengthen levee banks and clear and repair canals.

Every emergency service worker was deployed to help clean up the sodden state. Armies of unemployed men were despatched to such stricken towns as Koo Wee Rup. As they worked, they were assailed by heart-wrenching tales, such as that of farmer A.J. Gilchrist, who, having lost all his cattle in the flood, was cleaning up his once-submerged home and lit a fire in his kitchen to dry clothing, blankets and carpet. The fire got out of control and burned his house to the ground. Gilchrist was taken in by neighbours. Artists Hans Heysen, Frederick McCubbin, Arthur Streeton and fifty-seven others donated paintings to be auctioned with proceeds earmarked for the stricken. The paintings were among their finest. As one newspaper noted, 'There are no studio sweepings or unconsidered trifles for sale.'

Others were not so charitable. At Koo Wee Rup and Chelsea, and elsewhere, there was looting. Thieves ransacked abandoned homes and stole watches, jewellery and appliances that had been left behind by the occupants in their dash to safety. Some arrests were made.

The following year, 1935, the Royal Humane Society doled out a then-record number of bravery awards, most going to those who played their part during the great storm and flood of 1934. Within three years of the storm, parts of the Yarra River were stabilised and lined with limestone, and trees were planted to strengthen the banks. The Yarra, of course, would break its banks again, but the terrible scenes of 1934 have not been repeated.

CHAPTER 8

THE BROOME CYCLONE

26 MARCH 1935

From November to April every year, those who live and work on the north coast of Western Australia are on edge, for this is the cyclone season. More than 200 cyclones have been recorded in the region since recording of the events began in 1870.

On Christmas Eve, 1875, fifty-nine people died and several pearling luggers were sunk when a willy-willy assailed Exmouth Gulf. On 22 April 1887, some 140 men were drowned and eighteen luggers destroyed by a hurricane, and when not one but two cyclones crossed the Pilbara coast between 4 and 9 January 1894, Roebourne and nearby Cossack were battered, and the death toll was over forty. More than fifty lives were lost when a cyclone battered La Grange Bay and Broome on 26 and 27 April 1908, and that December another fifty-plus seamen died in a terrible tempest that extended from Broome and La Grange to Wallal.

Broome was again smashed by a hurricane on 19 November 1910. Forty died in that storm, whose winds gusted at an estimated 175 kilometres per hour. Twenty homes were destroyed, twenty seriously damaged and seventy partially damaged; thirty-four of the 300 pearling luggers in the region were sunk or wrecked, and some sixty-seven blown ashore. The schooner *Eclipse* was left a ruin on Cable Beach.

One of the most destructive cyclones in the nation's history occurred two years later, in March 1912. It crossed the coast near Balla Balla and destroyed numerous ships, including the *Koombana,* costing more than 150 lives. The most recent devastating cyclone occurred in April 2000 when ferocious rain and winds of up to 153 kilometres per hour battered Broome's upmarket Eco Beach Resort and lashed Thangoo and Yardoogarra Stations. Power was cut, but there were no fatalities.

Yet arguably the most devastating cyclone ever to strike the north of Western Australia attacked the historic and picturesque pearling town of Broome in March 1935.

The cyclone first came to notice as a storm that blew in from the sea on Monday, 25 March, and caused strong winds and rain in Broome and Derby. In the days prior there had been no sign of impending storm activity. But suddenly, on the Wednesday morning, the barometer plummeted and

Broome, particularly, was lashed by fierce winds and heavy driving rain. Reported the *West Australian*:

> Already Broome is assuming a desolate appearance, with many of its ornamental trees stripped of their foliage and deposits of leaves and rubbish everywhere. Several buildings in the Asiatic quarter [most of the pearl lugger crews and the divers were Asian] show signs of the strain and should the velocity of the wind increase, which seems almost certain, considerable damage will probably result. The residence of Mrs Errington, at the corner of Carnarvon Street and Napier terrace, appears to be on the verge of collapse.

There was worse to come – far worse. The storm that hit on 25 March was but a harbinger of a cyclone that at that time was lurking out to sea, and on 28 March, it advanced to the coast.

Cyclone warnings were issued and, as the sky turned a forbidding and lurid purple, the people of Broome and Derby took shelter, fearing the worst and hoping for the best. They got the former – their towns were devastated. Telegraph and telephone poles were knocked down by the 110 kilometre per hour westerly gale. Homes, including Mrs Errington's, and Low's ice works were destroyed. Houses, shops, offices and stables were damaged by the winds which ripped free corrugated iron roofs, verandas and awnings and flung them into the air or along the street. Trees were uprooted. Vessels were torn from their moorings and smashed on the beaches. Broome's four pubs – to the chagrin of the townsfolk – were badly battered. Up to 10 centimetres of sand, blown from the beach, lay thick upon the streets.

Although in December 1934 the Victorian branch of the Seamen's Union had warned of the need to install radio receivers in coastal vessels such as pearling luggers so they could be apprised of weather conditions, the estimated cost – £350 – was considered prohibitive by proprietors. So in March 1935, when the cyclone struck Broome and Derby and surrounds, no advance notice could be given to the captains of the twenty-six pearling luggers operating in the Lacepede Islands – off the coast between Broome and Derby – of what they were in for. All they had to rely on was the falling and rising of the barometer.

Pearling vessels in those days typically carried two divers (one of whom was usually the captain of the ship) and two tenders, and a crew of six. The divers wore heavy helmets and suits. Air was supplied by hand pump into the helmet by those manning the tenders. Most divers and crew were, as noted, 'Asiatics'. Occasionally, the shell openers – that is, those whose job it was to extricate the mother-of-pearl from the oyster shells collected by the divers – would be Caucasian. In the Depression, at the time of the cyclone of 1935, the pearling industry was on its knees, there not being much demand at the time for pearl jewellery. A lugger would cost around £1400 and the diving equipment about £500. It was a sign of the desperation of the times that luggers were forced to venture out during the treacherous hurricane season.

A diver whose lugger did ride out the cyclone and make it to Broome later testified:

> We were fishing off Barred Creek on Tuesday afternoon in very clear water and raising good quantities of shell [oyster shells], and the barometer began to fall, and we suggested to the other boats that they should make for Barred Creek. The other boats did not consider that the barometer drop was serious, and decided to wait until dawn on Wednesday morning. During the night and early morning, however, the blow struck them with terrific force. All boats immediately tried to make Barred Creek, but found this impossible, and had to put out sea anchors – a difficult task in the raging seas ... if they had left their pearling grounds some hours earlier they would have been able to make the creek and shelter.

When the storm hit, four luggers were able to avoid being driven out to sea and reach safety under their own steam. Two, the *B95* and the *Cleopatra*, were disabled and dismasted by the storm. Captain J. Eggleston of the passenger ship *Koolinda*, which eventually came to their aid, tells the story:

We left Broome at 12.30 p.m. on Monday [26 March], with the weather rather unsettled. We were off Cape Leveque at 5 a.m. on Tuesday, with the weather becoming much worse. I kept manoeuvring the vessel, sailing west of Leveque light, in hopes of the weather clearing at daylight. The weather grew worse. I endeavoured to get into King's Sound as I feared there was a cyclone about. At 7 a.m. on Tuesday I ordered the ship to be battened down and everything lashed. All hands turned to. At 8 a.m. the fresh gale struck the ship with continuous heavy rain, but at 8.40 we managed to check our position. At 1 p.m. we received advice that there was a willy-willy between Derby and Broome. I decided, owing to the lee shore, to put the ship out to sea. We went out at full speed. We met the whole gale that afternoon. The wind was blowing at between 80 and 90 miles an hour. The vessel was standing up magnificently. The ship's log read, 'whole gale, wind of hurricane force, almost continuous wind and rain squalls, high mountainous seas, heavy confused swells. The vessel shipping water and heavy spray over all' ...

At 7 p.m., we had crossed ahead of the centre of the cyclone, and then the gale slowly moderated. I manoeuvred on the outer edges of the cyclone for 24 hours and on Wednesday evening I set the ship back to Derby. The weather was still very bad but the worst had passed. At Thursday at 8.15 a.m. I was on the bridge when I saw an object on the troubled seas. We did not know that luggers had been in the cyclone. Through the glass I made out a lugger flying the reversed ensign, the sign of distress. I altered the course of the ship and proceeded to the lugger, about four miles away. The vessel was manoeuvred and oil pumped over the rough sea. A ship's lifeboat was sent away, in charge of the chief officer, Mr Sinclair. The lifeboat was very ably manned and the lugger was reached. It had been dismasted by the storm. While transferring the wrecked lugger crew to the lifeboat the chief officer was thrown overboard by the sea, but quickly got out of the water. The boat returned to the ship from the lugger with 10 cold and hungry men. They were given food and clothing and accommodated on the afterdeck.

This stricken vessel was the *B95*.

Early on Thursday afternoon, the *Koolinda* passed several pieces of floating wreckage and apparel and at 2.52 p.m. Eggleston and his shipmates sighted a dismasted lugger. They approached it and found it was the lugger *Cleopatra*, flying distress signals. Another eight men were rescued.

On Friday, 30 March, twenty pearling luggers were declared missing. On board were as many as 142 men. The *Koolinda*'s Captain Eggleston, during an extensive search for the vessels, reported seeing wreckage in the sea and a submerged lugger with its broken mast and cabin rising above the water. This time there were no survivors.

By then, the cyclone had abated, but, despite the best efforts of search craft, there was no sign of the missing boats or any of the men ... alive, anyway. Some bodies had been sighted in the water or washed onto the shore, a number bearing the dreadful marks of shark attack. The waters were shark-infested, for it was the time of year when turtles hatched their eggs.

Searchers followed footprints up the sand on one of the Lacepede islands to a grisly find: the body of a man covered in wounds that were the result of either being dashed upon rocks or mauled by sharks. He had struggled from the sea, staggered up the beach, then fallen and died in the scrub.

More happily, a Japanese crewman appeared with a story of how he had been swept overboard from a lugger by a wave and washed up on an island. There he had survived for five days on oysters and birds eggs.

After the cyclone passed, a Father Worms arrived from Beagle Bay, about 120 kilometres north of Broome, with the news that the settlement had suffered catastrophic punishment. From Tuesday afternoon to Wednesday afternoon, over 500 millimetres of rain had fallen on Beagle Bay. The roof of the Roman Catholic Mission there had been blown off, as had the roofs of the children's dormitory and the leper hospital. No building remained unscathed. The powering winds had uprooted baobab trees and coconut trees, many of them over fifty years old, and stripped the bark from gum trees.

In time, as a direct result of the 1935 disaster, radio sets were installed in a number – but by no means all – of the pearling luggers. By the mid 1930s, the heyday of pearling was long past. The years 1880–1914, boom times for pearling in Roebuck Bay, are considered pearling's golden age. Australians, Europeans, Japanese, Chinese, Malays and Koepangers swarmed to the beautiful port with its colourful rock formations and cobalt blue seas with a fervour equalled in Australia only by those caught up in the great gold rush. Then the Depression reduced the demand for pearls, and with World War II many of the Japanese divers and crew – though innocent of conspiring against Australia – were interned as a precaution in indentured camps as security risks. The invention of plastic buttons in the 1950s made mother-of-pearl largely redundant. Only the cultured pearl industry remains viable today, with Broome supplying around 60 per cent of the world's best quality cultured South Sea pearls.

CHAPTER 9

BONDI'S BLACK SUNDAY

6 FEBRUARY 1938

That high summer Sunday dawned hot and windless over Sydney. The sixth day of February 1938 would be a stinker. Sydneysiders, along with many in town to see the Empire Games Opening Ceremony at the Sydney Cricket Ground the day before, converged on Bondi Beach – then as now a graceful crescent-shaped beach with fine white sands – in cars, buses, trams and on foot. The seas were rough up and down the coast, which did not deter the sweltering hordes from taking a dip. Around 35 000 were at the beach that day. Recalled one Bondi lifesaver in the days that followed:

> It was a peculiar and tricky surf. People who understand surfing could handle it alright. The waves were fairly ordinary dumping ones, with a heavy curling crest on them. They were the sort one either has to dive under or sink down to the bottom until they passed. There seemed to be a terrific tow to the waves.

Some seventy-four people – a record number – were pulled from the roiling surf by lifesavers before lunch.

By early afternoon at Bondi, with the temperature edging 40 degrees Celsius, you could barely see the sand for sunbakers soaking up the rays and waiting for a surf carnival of lifesavers to start. There were around 750 bathers in the water, frolicking and catching waves between the red and yellow safety flags which had been speared into the sand 80 metres apart right in front of the pavilion in the centre of the beach. About 250 of the swimmers were standing on a sandbank 30 metres out, waiting for a breaker to roll in from out the back and whisk them in to shore.

Just after 3 p.m, the rough sea quietened. Many would later describe the sudden stilling of the waves as 'eerie'.

Then, without warning, three – or some eyewitnesses swear they saw four – freak 4-metre dumpers, described by one onlooker as 'like tidal waves', sprang up and crashed upon the beach in rapid succession. The piggy-backing mass of water surged 30 metres up the sand, knocking down toddlers and beach umbrellas, engulfing clothes and towels, and laying waste to scores of sandcastles. Then all that water rushed back to the sea, colliding with incoming breakers and causing a huge rip. The mighty backwash sucked those who had been standing upon the sandbank into a deep and raging channel and swept them out to sea.

Terrible scenes ensued, scenes that those who witnessed them never forgot. Panic-stricken swimmers flailed hysterically in the water, powerless to swim to shore against its pull. Some were dragged underwater and battered and tumbled, as if in a giant washing machine, by the mountainous waves and turbulent white water. Others found themselves 200 metres offshore and way out of their depth. They fought for their lives, gasping for breath, screaming, crying, praying, climbing upon each other in an effort to stay afloat. 'The whole thing was so tragically sudden that one hardly knows what happened,' Alfred Scott Moore of Kings Cross told the *Sydney Morning Herald* later that day.

> I was on the sandbank with the water up to my waist when I remarked to another surfer that I was thinking of leaving the water. The water seemed to be pulling us out. Shortly afterwards there was a huge backwash from the shore and it crashed into an oncoming wave. There was a terrific impact and we were all taken out 100 yards seaward, and all of us were struggling in deep water. We were swept out like debris.

On the beach, people rose from the sand and stood stunned, all eyes on the pandemonium in the water. Appalled onlookers called for their loved ones.

The sixty lifesavers on the beach, most of whom were from Bondi or North Bondi clubs, responded calmly and swiftly and plunged in to rescue the drowning. Surf boats being useless in the big seas, the lifesavers swam, or manned the seven reels that had been set up on the beach for the carnival, or paddled rubber floats, surf skis and surfboards. Many members of the public – a number of them, incredibly, non-swimmers – risked their lives and dived in too. As soon as they brought a floundering bather to shore, they returned to save others. Police from Bondi and other stations took up positions on the sand and summoned doctors and ambulances to the scene. Medical centres were set up on the sand, manned by doctors and volunteers with medical supplies and oxygen equipment. Bondi surf club was quickly transformed into an emergency ward.

Tales of great heroism are legion. Bondi Surf Club captain Carl Jeppeson, doing his work without equipment, single-handedly rescued six. New Zealand swimming champion Ena Stockley, who was one of those swept off the sandbank, swam to save a child who was disappearing under the water and on taking the spluttering infant to the beach returned to the water to save more. She was nearly drowned herself when an elderly man, in a blind panic, grasped her wrist and would not let go.

Kenneth Byrne of Glebe recounted how he had been swept away 'in a flash ... My head was more underwater than above it. I thought I was done until my hands touched a lifeline and I began to pull myself to the shore. I was exhausted when someone grabbed me and I remembered no more until I was brought to the club house.' Harry Hoare of Balmain's efforts to stay afloat were hampered by another swimmer who clutched him around the neck in a desperate bid to save himself. 'I managed to shake off his hold on me.'

The lifesavers attested to the many frenzied men who seized them and dragged them down, who screamed and cried and begged to be saved; and to the women who remained cool and courageous as they helped each other and waited to be saved. Lifesaver Arthur Elm told how he had swum near a group of men, among the furthest out from shore, and five of them had grabbed him and refused to let go.

> The girls were all right, but some of the men seemed to go mad. I was trying to take the belt to a youngster who was right out, but I didn't get the chance. As I went by dozens yelled for help and tried to grab me. I told them to hang onto the rope as soon as I had got it out but they didn't wait. They made for me. I didn't think I had a chance when they all came at me. One grabbed me by the neck and two others caught me by one arm, another held me around the waist and another seized my leg. I hit the man who had me by the neck. I managed to hit him on the chin and he let go. I had to

The doctors and nurses of the Influenza Administration Committee were at the ready in Sydney during the 1919 Spanish influenza pandemic.
© *Newspix*

Time-honoured sanctuaries such as churches were inundated, along with homes, farms and cities, when floods submerged much of Tasmania in April 1929.
© *Tasmanian Archive and Heritage Office*

Survivors observed the water that had engulfed their town from the banks of the South Esk, in Longford, Tasmania.
© *Tasmanian Archive and Heritage Office*

Sydney's Bondi Beach resembled a battlefield on 6 February 1938, after a series of large waves swept hundreds of swimmers out to sea. Heroic lifesavers rescued 245; five perished.

A devastated Darwin home owner returns to pick through the wreckage of his home, one of thousands laid waste by Cyclone Tracy in Darwin on Christmas Day, 1974.

Despair is etched on the face of Mrs M. Gatis and her daughter, Nectaria, 3, who with other daughter Poppy, 1, were among the more than 10,000 residents airlifted from Darwin Airport after Cyclone Tracy razed the city.
© AP via AAP Photo

On 18 January 1977, a train collided with an overhead bridge at Sydney's Granville Railway Station, bringing the 200-tonne concrete bridge crashing down. The death toll was 83, and more than 200 were injured.
© *Blue Mountains City Library – Local Studies Collection*

Thirteen died and 160 were injured when an earthquake levelled most of Newcastle, NSW, on 28 December 1989.
© *Newspix*

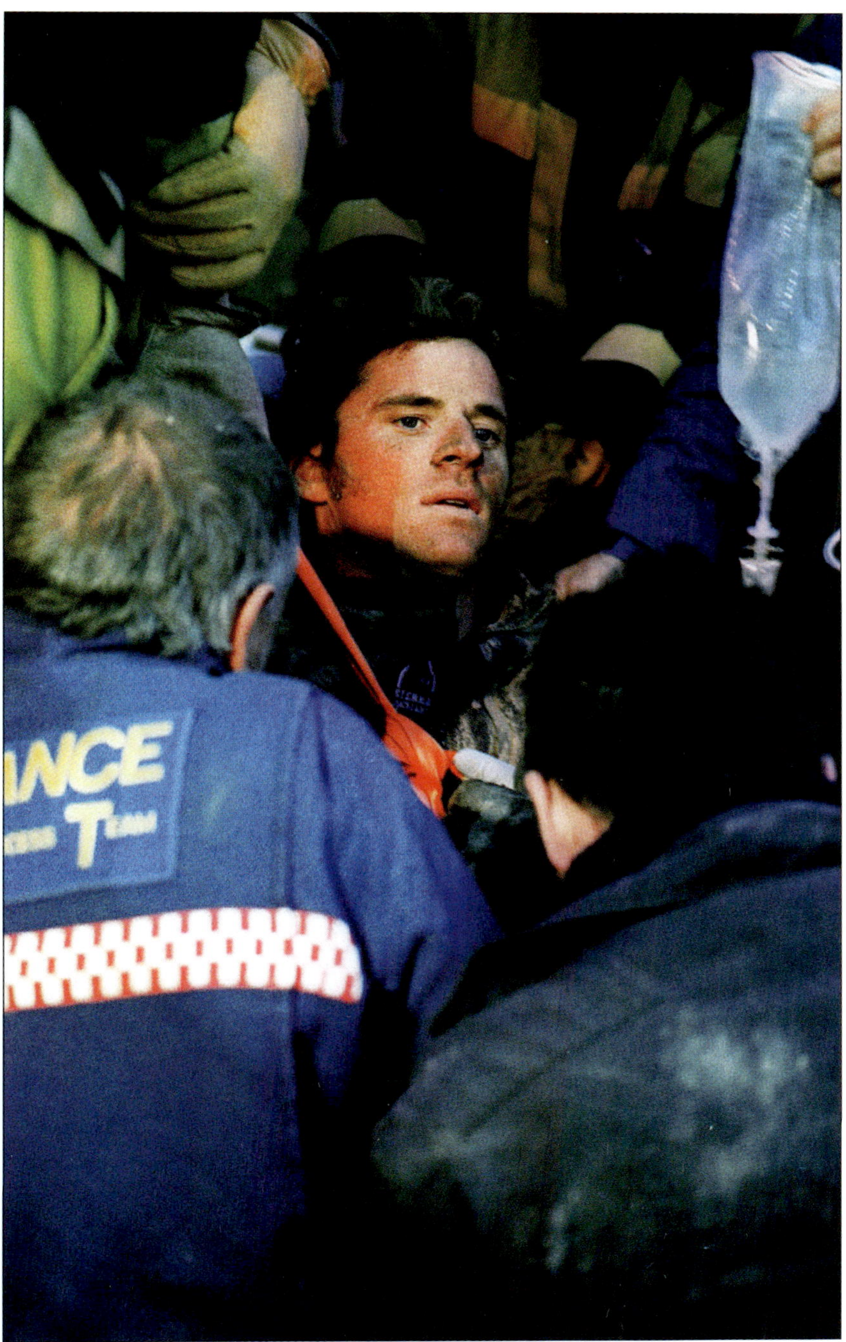

After the Thredbo landslide on 30 July 1997, miracle survivor Stuart Diver is extricated from beneath the rubble of his ski lodge where he had lain for 65 hours beside the body of his wife, Sally.

A patchwork of tarpaulins covered Sydney after Australia's most damaging hailstorm, on 21 April 1999, smashed roofs, windows, cars, trees and gardens.
© AFP via AAP/Torsten Blackwood

There were no survivors when, on 7 May 2005, a Fairchild Metroliner Commuter plane crashed into a mountain near the Lockhart river on Queensland's Cape York Peninsula.
© AAP Image

Firestorm at Bunyip State Park, west of Melbourne. Despite the sterling work of emergency services and citizen volunteers, much of Victoria was turned to cinders by raging bushfires in January and February 2009 that killed 173 people.
© *William West/AFP/Getty Images*

Fatima Aqhlaqi mourns her brother-in-law at a memorial service at Sydney's Rookwood Cemetery for asylum seekers who drowned when ramshackle Indonesian fishing boat SIEV-221 sank off the coast of Christmas Island on 15 December 2010.
© *Newspix*

Large swathes of Queensland, including the city of Brisbane and its suburbs, were inundated by brown floodwaters in December 2010 and January 2011.
© AFP via AAP/Torsten Blackwood

In the tradition of Australians faced with disaster, citizens rose to the occasion during the Queensland floods. Here, despite rapidly rising water, volunteers carry sandbags across a submerged street in Rosalie, west of Brisbane.
© Newspix

> do it. But for that I would have drowned myself, and some of the others too.

Carl Jeppeson refused to single out lifesavers who had distinguished themselves, saying:

> There were many heroes. Everyone did his job. All the men who were on the beach went straight into the water and started swimming towards the helpless people. There were at least 200 people in trouble at the same time. We saw a succession of four huge waves, and then out went the people. We were preparing to start a surf race with three teams of 15 each: the relieving patrol was just about to take over from the patrol which had been on the beach.
>
> But for the fact that there were so many lifesavers on the beach, many more would have drowned. As it was, there were about 70 ... and they all went in at once. There were seven reels out but most of us had to go out without a line. Many went out on surf floats and these proved valuable, for as many as five people were able to hang onto them and keep their heads above water. A surf ski which went out tipped over, but seven people were able to cling to it, and were dragged ashore.
>
> It is hard to look back now on what it was like out there in that surf. People were sinking all around us. We were doing our best to hold them up to get them to surf floats, and to stop their panic. It was our Black Sunday.

The magazine *Surfline* noted in a 1982 article about Black Sunday:

> There had been no precedent set in all the years of surfing for such an awful emergency. No patrolman had ever before seen the seas so crowded with people drowning. There was no time to ponder ways and means, for while men were thinking, people would be drowning. In that afternoon was reaped in fullest measure the harvest of the years of training. In spontaneous, automatic action,

> ensured by the tireless, long hours of drilling to which all had been subjected, the lifesavers carried out their duty.
>
> The beach, within the space of a few minutes, resembled a battleground. Prone bodies were everywhere. The unhurried, measured pumping that would give most of them life again went on continuously.

Although Carl Jeppeson would name no heroes, and Sergeant Gorman, whose job it was to identify those who had displayed bravery, said, 'It's impossible to mention even a fraction of those whose actions saved lives', Jeppeson's name, along with those of fellow lifesavers Tom Meagher, Aub Laidlaw, John Cox, Basil McDonald, Asher Hart and Arthur Elm, and police officers Ranch, Walsh and Bassingthwaite, were mentioned repeatedly in rescue accounts.

Jeppeson said later, 'This is the hardest day's work I have ever known. The [lifesavers] were splendid in the face of great difficulties, not the least of which was the well-meant hindrance of the crowd.'

Added beach inspector Tom Meagher:

> Over 20 of them grabbed a new line on which a number of people were clinging, and their strong pulling caused it to break. Others became entangled in lines, and some kept talking to the men as they worked. During resuscitation the crowd had to be kept back by a number of men who formed a human chain.

In twenty minutes of frenetic activity, in what remains to this day the biggest mass rescue in Australia's history, some 245 people were rescued. Of these, five were carried unconscious from the surf and revived with artificial respiration, sixty were assisted onto the sand suffering immersion and shock, and 150 were unharmed save for exhaustion. One of these was 15-year-old Mary Wein, who would become Lady Mary Fairfax, wife of media tycoon Sir Warwick Fairfax.

Under cover on the sand were the lifeless forms of the drowned Charles Saur of Darlinghurst, in his fifties, Ronald McGregor, 21, of Bondi,

Leslie Potter, 19, of Bondi and Bernard Byrne, 34, of Earlwood. The body of Michael Taylor, 33, of Surry Hills, washed to shore at Bondi on Thursday, 10 February.

For the next week, police patrolled the shores of Bondi, Tamarama, Bronte and Coogee beaches, to be on hand if any further bodies washed ashore.

Charles 'Sweet' Saur's gallantry cost him his life. As the German-born chef was being dragged out by the undertow, he saw a small girl in dire straits a few metres away. He swam to her and, although failing from exhaustion himself, he held her head above the water with one arm while signalling for help with the other. Saur managed to grasp a surf line and with super-human effort he hauled himself and the now-unconscious girl in to shore and safety. There he collapsed and could not be revived.

Marshall Dyer, an American doctor who was at Bondi that day to take a moving picture of the surf carnival, and whose help tending the rescued and keeping the crowd under control was invaluable, was interviewed by reporters and heaped praise on the lifesavers. He declared:

> I have never seen, and I never expect to see again, such magnificent work as was done by those lifesavers. It is the most incredible work of love in the world. Just imagine those men all going into the water without a moment's hesitation, risking their lives, and all for love. In America, all our lifesavers are paid … Yesterday's rescue was the most amazing I have ever seen … It was a scene I shall never forget, and when I get back to the United States I will tell them about your magnificent surf men. There are no men like them in the world.

Of the many tragedies of 6 February 1938, few were more heart-rending than that of the Taylor family. On that blazing hot Sunday morning Michael Taylor had arrived at the beach with his 13-year-old son, Jack. Both were anxious for a cooling swim. At about 2.30 Michael left Jack on the sand and, wearing a bright red costume, dived into the water. Soon after came the freak waves and an afternoon of chaos. At 5.30, when the swimmers had been treated and the four bodies taken away in an ambulance, Jack was walking up and down the beach, calling his father's name. Not knowing his father's fate, the boy returned home to Surry Hills. The family's worst fears were raised by a 7 p.m. radio news bulletin that said clothing and belongings had been left unclaimed in a dressing shed. Mrs Taylor contacted the police and, at Bondi Police Station, identified her missing husband's belongings: a pair of grey striped trousers, a white cotton singlet with a Gowings tag, a grey striped shirt with gilt sleeve links, a pair of tan shoes with a David Jones brand inside and a pair of grey socks. Search boats were sent out to try to locate Michael Taylor's body, without success.

On 25 February, City Coroner Oram called the Black Sunday catastrophe the most tragic experience in the history of Sydney's beaches and gave 'accidental drowning' as the cause of the deaths of Taylor, Saur, Potter, McGregor and Byrne. As well as the lifesavers, he made special mention of the work of officers from Eastern Suburbs Ambulance Service and Drs Ping, Hardie and McKellar, and lauded a Mr Gatley of the Esplanade Café for providing hot water, coffee and tea.

In the end, rather than recognising individuals for their heroic acts on Black Sunday, the Surf Life Saving Association of Australia honoured all the lifesavers on the beach that day with a special meritorious award.

CHAPTER 10

THE TAA FOKKER FRIENDSHIP DISASTER

10 JUNE 1960

It should have been the most routine of flights. Just after 5 p.m. on Friday, 10 June 1960, the one-year-old TAA twin-Rolls-Royce-engine Fokker Friendship passenger jet, christened the *Abel Tasman* and piloted by Captain F.C. Pollard, departed Brisbane, bound for Mackay in Queensland's north. En route, Flight 538, as it was designated, set down at Maryborough and Rockhampton to pick up passengers. At the latter airport seven adults and nine boys from Rockhampton Grammar School joined the flight, returning to their homes in Mackay to celebrate the Queen's Birthday long weekend. For one lad, Max Barclay, the journey was a ninth birthday gift from his parents. In all, there were twenty-nine on board, including, as well as the schoolboys, John O'Grady, the United States Consul in Queensland, and A.E. Cole, Director of the Queensland Tourist Bureau. The aircraft took off from Rockhampton at 7.52 p.m. for the final short hop of the journey.

It was 8.17 when Captain Pollard was advised by Mackay air traffic controller E.W. Miskell that shallow ground fog to the height of 6 metres had enveloped the airport and it was to be closed until the fog dissipated. With plenty of fuel on board, Pollard radioed Miskell that, rather than divert to Townsville – for he had ample fuel to do so – he would circle Mackay at 4000 metres in case visibility improved. It seemed a reasonable plan. Apart from the pocket of fog and some cloud hanging over the airport, the night was clear and bright, thanks to a bright moon. There was little wind and the sea was a millpond. The plane made a couple of attempts to land – the pilot presumably believing conditions had improved – but each time poor visibility due to the clouds and fog thwarted the attempt.

Nearing 10 p.m., Miskell reported to Captain Pollard, who was still circling the airport, that the fog was at last lifting. Pollard replied that he would begin his approach to the airport for landing. 'Roger, tower, will commence let down to approach on runway 32.' Miskell reiterated the weather conditions, and Pollard acknowledged the message. Miskell then advised Pollard that the temperature on the ground at Mackay Airport was 13 degrees Celsius. But this time there was no reply. Miskell repeated the message. Again, silence. It was 10.02 p.m. At 10.10, Miskell, now confounded and deeply concerned, organised a search and rescue mission. Announced R.G. Cochrane, TAA's Queensland manager:

> We have lost contact with the aircraft. Full emergency procedures have been set in motion and launches and aircraft are on the way to the area above which the Fokker Friendship was circling. We will not be releasing the names of the people on board until their next of kin have been notified. We are now in the process of notifying them.

There were reports that a 'dull explosion' was heard by Mackay residents between 10.10 and 10.15. Reported camper Vincent Bricknell, 'The fog was like pea soup ... We heard the aircraft circling for at least half an hour. Later we heard a thud which sounded like an explosion of gelignite. There was only the one sound.' Fisherman Albert Christensen reported that he had heard the plane circling, and then its engines had stopped. Soon after he had heard 'an explosion and then the shrieking of metal being torn to pieces'. Eileen Ford told how, while watching the plane circling above, she had had a premonition that it would crash. 'I called out to my family, "If I call out, you come running ... This plane is in trouble." Then I heard a swoosh and a distant bang and I said, "She has blown up!"' Later, Ford learned that her brother, Dudley Phillips, was a passenger on the doomed aircraft.

At 3 a.m. on the Saturday morning, the mystery of the disappearance of Flight 538 was solved in the most tragic way, when a motor launch in the search party located eight bodies, some of which had been mauled by sharks, and wreckage, including schoolbooks and caps, luggage, passenger seats, clothes and cabin furnishings floating in the sea 5 nautical miles east of Mackay Airport, between Round Top Island and Flat Top Island. Other boats and aircraft came to the scene and found no survivors. Waiting on the Mackay tourist pier for news was a 3000-strong crowd, including many distraught and weeping relatives of the passengers. As the launches returned to the dock, bodies were transferred from them to hearses.

The bodies of Captain Pollard and his co-pilot G.L. Davis were later found floating side by side. Captain Pollard's watch had stopped at seven minutes and 30 seconds past 10.

It wasn't till Sunday at 4.20 p.m. that the two major sections of the aircraft, and nineteen bodies, were located by Navy vessel HMAS *Warrego* in 12 metres of water 3 nautical miles south-east of the airport. The fuselage was clearly visible in the crystal blue water. Tossed like corks in 5-metre waves, the *Warrego* and the HMAS *Kimbla* raised the wreckage after divers had performed the grisly task of extricating the bodies. The salvage operation took nearly two weeks.

Circling sharks hampered the operation. Captain Sanderson of the *Warrego* posted snipers with .303 rifles on the deck after two grey nurse sharks, one 4 metres long and the other 2 metres, menaced divers.

A diver later spoke of what he saw when he descended into the depths.

> A big section of the sandy floor is ploughed up like a paddock. The airliner must have hit the water at terrific speed because 40 ft [sic] of water did not cushion the impact. When bits of wreckage hit the seabed they ploughed up great furrows. Only the red-painted fin of the tail assembly was sticking out of the sand at an angle of 45 degrees. A few feet of fuselage was attached to the tail section. We found the shattered blades of both propellers which had torn away from the engines.

In the wake of the crash, Captain Pollard's decision to circle over Mackay Airport was questioned. Railed Queensland senator E.B. Maher:

> In my experience it is risky enough descending through heavy fog during the daytime, but it is an unnecessary risk to impose on passengers and crew by night. Could not the aircraft have been diverted back to Rockhampton, or on to Townsville? Can anyone imagine anything sillier than aircraft circling around idly for hours, burning up fuel and fraying the nerves of passengers and crew [rather than] land somewhere safe and wait for favourable weather conditions?

Senator Maher, however, was rebuked by a Department of Civil Aviation spokesman who countered that the *Abel Tasman* was following accepted procedure when it circled Mackay, waiting for the fog to lift. 'Had it not lifted,' he said, 'the aircraft still would have had enough fuel to fly on to Townsville.'

A Board of Accident Inquiry, chaired by Mr Justice Spicer, Chief Judge of the Commonwealth Industrial Court, was commissioned. It commenced its investigation on 4 October. The members of the inquiry board, including nine leading barristers and among them four Queen's Counsel, examined the salvaged wreckage which had been reassembled, as best as could be accomplished, in a Mackay Harbour Board shed. They flew over the flight path taken by Flight 538 in its final minutes, and inspected the navigational aids, meteorological and communications systems at Mackay Airport, and the air traffic systems in place there.

When the inquiry concluded, on 10 November, the board offered no definitive reason why the plane pitched into the sea. There was no evidence of engine failure or metal fatigue, nor of any structural defects. There was no evidence of fire, explosion or act by any person on board that may have brought the plane down. The inquiry findings also refuted some mooted possible causes, such as that the altimeter – the device that measures altitude – may have malfunctioned; that Captain Pollard might have misread the altimeter, leading to pilot error (unlikely considering Pollard's lengthy experience); or that the crew might have confused moonlight on the water for the airstrip.

Nor did it support TAA's technical services engineering superintendent Frank McMullen, who had stated that perhaps while attempting to land, Captain Pollard had opted for a low flight path, hoping to keep the airstrip in sight below the cloud layer, 'but was deceived by the difficulty in assessing height over a glassy sea and put the left wing-tip into the water turning onto the runway'.

In 1960, black box flight recorders were still on the drawing board. They were the brainchild of Australian aeronautical scientist David Warren, whose father had perished in an aircraft that crashed into Bass Strait in 1934. As a result of the Mackay crash, the Board of

Accident Inquiry strongly recommended that the devices be installed in Australian commercial aircraft. Today, all Australian-registered aircraft with a maximum take-off weight greater than 5700 kilograms must be equipped with two black boxes: a flight data recorder and a cockpit voice recorder.

In the Queen's Birthday Honours List announced in June the following year, a number of those involved in the salvaging of the *Abel Tasman* were awarded gallantry medals. The *Warrego*'s acting commander Noel Sanderson, who was in charge of the operation, was awarded the OBE for his 'exceptional skill and devotion to duty in the planning and direction of this difficult task'. MBEs were presented to Lieutenant Alan Wright of the Royal Navy, who led the combined diving team and 'personally undertook the most hazardous and difficult tasks', and Sub-Lieutenant William Roberts, who had been 'faced not only by the normal hazards of diving in the open sea but also by the threat of vicious sharks and the continual danger of fouling air hoses on jagged edges of the wreckage'. Others honoured were Able-Seaman Harold Bingham, Electrical Artificer First Class George Jones, and Engine Room Artificer Fourth Class Albert Pollard.

In the grounds of Rockhampton Grammar School there is a memorial garden where a plaque commemorates the boys lost on Flight 538. The names of the lads are listed upon it. In 2010, to mark the fiftieth anniversary of the disaster, the families and friends of those who were killed gathered for a memorial ceremony at Mackay's Far Beach, near where the aircraft crashed. Prayers were said while all present looked out to sea, many through misty eyes, and more than thirty wreaths were laid. A Tiger Moth bi-plane soared high over the beach and dropped a wreath into the blue ocean. It was a quiet and poignant occasion where, it was written, 'the memories of loved ones floated on the cool, crisp breeze.'

On 26 May 2010, Margaret Clark of Brisbane, a former air hostess, wrote a letter to the *Australian*:

> As I remember, June 11, 1960, dawned as any other winter morning in Brisbane. I was in no hurry to begin the day. Then the

morning newspaper arrived and when it was placed in front of me, it became startlingly obvious that this was not to be like any other day in my life. The headlines said a Fokker Friendship was missing off the Queensland coast near Mackay. TAA aircraft don't crash, I thought. When news came through on the radio that wreckage had been found, I had to face the truth. Flight 538 had indeed crashed into the sea on the morning of June 10. I could have been on that flight. Perhaps I should have been. I have wrestled with the 'why' of this for the rest of my life.

Like many other young women in the 1950s, I decided that I would like to become an air hostess (as they were then known). My application to Trans Australia Airways (TAA) was successful and I became an air hostess based in Brisbane. Every three weeks, Flight 538, Brisbane to Mackay, would appear on my roster. Three weeks previously, I had been on the crew of that flight with one of the hostesses who died in the crash. It was therefore possible that either one of us could have been on that flight. Why not me? Is our life all mapped out for us? Or was it pure chance that my life was spared?

This day became a day like no other, as I was one of the hostesses rostered on Flight 538 that afternoon, the day after the crash in which 29 people (including the captain, first officer and two hostesses) died. The flight proceeded, touching down at Maryborough and Rockhampton as normal. We then proceeded north towards Mackay, where apparently weather conditions were exactly the same as they had been on the previous [evening]: dangerous for landing. The captain therefore decided to circle over the water. This was most disturbing, as looking out the windows one could see the lights below where the plane had gone down into the sea the previous day and where the searchers were still looking for bodies.

It was then that what had happened became a reality. Our aircraft circled and circled the wreck, giving all on board the chance to reflect on the fragility of life. I was fortunate enough to live on and to try to learn something from this tragedy. I realised that it was probably pure chance that I flew on June 11, not June 10. I was given the opportunity to learn to value the present moment but, as I am human, I forget this simple truth quite often.

CHAPTER 11

THE COLLAPSE OF THE WEST GATE BRIDGE

15 OCTOBER 1970

Venice has its Bridge of Sighs. Melbourne has its Bridge of Tears.

'On Thursday the 15th of October, 1970, between ten to and five to twelve noon,' said one eyewitness, a retired farmer who had taken a great interest in the building of Melbourne's new $42 million West Gate Bridge, 'I was sitting on a seat under the shelter of the viewing area on the south side of the West Gate Bridge, eating my lunch. I heard a few taps from a hammer on the bridge, [and] about five seconds later a loud noise similar to the breaking of a steel shaft. I just gazed across the bridge between the two piers, and all of a sudden ... on the north side of the bridge I saw the bridge starting to subside, then on the south side in the middle section I saw the bridge subsiding also. [Then] on the north side of the western section of the bridge ... I saw a small "V" of light come as the middle of the bridge kept moving outwards, then the western edge of the bridge fell and I watched it until it was about a third of the way to the ground, then I turned my eyes to the eastern edge of the bridge in time to hear the half girder land on the ground. The eastern pier appeared to hold for a moment, I would say about two seconds, then the pier began to fall towards the river.'

When work commenced, the West Gate Bridge was touted as Melbourne's answer to the Sydney Harbour Bridge, a sleek and graceful eight-lane arch – once described as a graceful and sinuous white snake – spanning the muddy marshes at the Yarra River's mouth at Spotswood. It would be 53 metres high, 2585 metres long and 37 metres wide and have twenty-seven pylons. The main section, which crossed the water, would comprise five steel spans. The middle three sections would be supported by cables stretching from steel towers that had been constructed on top of the concrete pylons.

A few weeks before the bridge collapsed on 15 October 1970, ultimately killing thirty-five workers, Jack Hindshaw, chief engineer for the bridge designer Freeman Fox, discovered that the fourth and fifth of the eight prefabricated box sections which formed two halves of the first box girder span high on the upper decking were misaligned: there was a camber difference, with one box section 11.3 centimetres lower than the other. To compensate, and save time, instead of lowering the two at-fault sections back to the ground and correcting the problem, the decision was taken by construction company John Holland Constructions Pty Ltd (JHC) to load the higher box section with a mass of heavy material, or kentledge. Ten cube-shaped 8-tonne concrete blocks happened to be on site from a previous job, and these were used to lower the higher section to the level of the other section. When the two sections were finally made to align, bolts were inserted to hold them together.

The remedy was a failure. It took only a week or two for the inner upper panel around joints 4 and 5 to buckle. Noted Hindshaw in his journal, 'Obvious overstress due to concrete kentledge.'

Freeman Fox construction experts, with Hindshaw in the vanguard, decided on 14 October to correct the major buckle by loosening thirty-seven of the bolts connecting the two mismatched sections. They believed that this would allow the sections to settle into place.

On 15 October, at around 8 a.m., the bolts were unfastened. The engineers were relieved to see that the buckle disappeared. By 11 a.m., however, the buckle was back, bigger than before. And the steel had changed from its normal rusty red to blue, indicating that the joint was now under terrible strain. Hindshaw, who had been summoned to the site by section engineer Ward, noted that because of the pressure a steel plate within section five had twisted inwards. Now new buckles were appearing. They had spread from the inner upper panel to the adjacent two outer upper panels. Ward and other witnesses later said that at this stage they felt 'a gentle settlement' of the north half span of the bridge.

Noting the workmen clambering over the structure, Hindshaw was heard to wonder aloud whether he should take the men off the bridge. He must have decided not to, because no order to evacuate the bridge was given.

Nearing midday, as Hindshaw looked on in increasing alarm at the escalating buckling at the junction of box sections four and five, there came a terrifying rumbling and creaking. Huge flakes of rust peeled from the twisting steel with a pinging sound; there was the escalating screech of metal grinding on metal. Hindshaw cried out to his men to get off the bridge. Some succeeded in doing so, but not Hindshaw himself. Then the joint snapped and the whole 2000-tonne steel section that it was supporting – along with Hindshaw and other men, a supporting pylon 'which tottered and fell like a stick', a 60-tonne crane, oil drums, heavy construction equipment and work shacks – plummeted 45 metres with a roar 'like thunder'.

Hindshaw and most of the men taken with the mass down to the Yarra waters and muddy banks were killed instantly, or would die in the ensuing days of their terrible injuries. Killed too were members of the day shift who were eating lunch in shacks that were crushed by thousands of tonnes of steel and concrete.

While horrified workmates scrambled in the mud, trying with crow bars, shovels and their bare hands to wrest those colleagues who were still alive free from the mud and the water, ambulance officers and doctors, police, the fire brigade and emergency services teams with oxyacetylene cutters and cranes were speeding to the scene, sirens screaming like banshees. Harbour Trust divers searched the depths of the Yarra for bodies. Priests came to administer the last rites to the dead and dying. Blood was supplied by the Red Cross for transfusions and four hospitals were placed on full alert and told to expect a rush of patients. Distraught loved ones of the workers crowded around the scene. Rescue and news helicopters buzzed overhead like dragonflies. Messages of comfort were sent by the Queen, Pope Paul VI, the Prime Ministers of Britain, Canada and New Zealand, and Australian Prime Minister John Gorton. Said State Opposition leader Clyde Holding, close to tears, 'It is the worst thing I have ever seen.'

Incredible tales emerged. Two men jumped 70 metres from the toppling pylon. One survived when he fell into viscous mud; the other was decapitated. Four men having lunch and poring over plans in a shack on the river bank were crushed by falling debris and their bodies were found where they sat, the plans, largely untouched, spread out before them.

Boilermaker Nino di Crea missed work that fateful day because he was unwell. He drove to the scene of destruction and cursed the unfairness that he was still alive, while his best friends were not.

Two days before the collapse, Roy Deveraux filmed a group of his fellow workers hard at work on the bridge with his home movie camera.

All died. Now he was left to watch their smiling faces as they waved at him from their eyrie high above the Yarra, happily oblivious to the horror that would befall them.

'All I can remember was a crash then burning and I was falling through the air and praying as I went down. Then someone was pulling me out of the water,' recalled Desmond Gibson, 29, who was at work on the top span when it collapsed. Though suffering broken ribs, bruises and burns, he sat up in his bed at Prince Henry's Hospital and relived his terrifying ordeal.

> I was working with a drill about 190 ft up, when I heard a crunch. The bridge opened up and I fell backwards ... then found myself in the Yarra. I was lying there, looking up to where the bridge should have been, but instead it was under me. Some of the fellows were talking when we started work. They said they had a feeling. They said, 'Gee, it could go.' Then I had a feeling, you know, just a feeling. And it did go. God, all I know is I don't want to go back to bridge work.

Rigger Frank Piermarini, 34, was interviewed by a reporter from the *Age* in his ward at Royal Melbourne Hospital. He had ridden the falling bridge to the ground, and said:

> By some grace of God I was spared. What of the others? What has happened to them? So many children won't be seeing their fathers again. At first I felt that the bridge was shaking but thought it was my imagination and kept on working. Then the whole damn thing sagged in the middle. I could see daylight through the enormous cracks in the concrete. The noise was tremendous.

He could hear his Italian workmates crying out,

> Che succede? [What's happening?] Mamma Mia, che succede? As I tried to scramble out, the whole world seemed to go into a massive slide. Everything became black and I thought I was finished. I was

> thrown from side to side as the bridge crumbled. Images of my wife and child kept flashing through my mind. Those seconds seemed like hours. God, how I prayed. I cannot remember hitting the ground. When I came to, I found myself deep in thick oil and slush. There were bodies everywhere. Some bodies had been mutilated beyond recognition. Some men were unrecognisable.'

One boilermaker's assistant who rode the span down to the river and survived told of his traumatic experience in a deposition to the Royal Commission investigating how and why the West Gate Bridge collapsed. He had been descending the scaffold on the span on which he had been working to have his lunch

> when the span I was standing on slowly started to sink down ... I held on to the scaffold and it seemed like 12 seconds until the span crashed into the river. I don't know if I was knocked over inside the box, but after the span hit the bottom I was covered in mud, blood was running down from a cut on my head and I was standing up with a scaffolding tube wrapped around my neck. I saw a fire about 15–20 feet from me. I don't know what was on fire. All the steel was twisted. A man I didn't know was a short distance from me and was screaming for help ... and then I didn't hear any more. I could see the sky through a gap in the steel above me and about five minutes later some men came but they couldn't get me out until some time later. The people pulled me out on a rope. I am very lucky to be alive.

As was another boilermaker's assistant who was called to the Commission. He recalled how at about 11.45 on 15 October he was in the bolt shed on span 10–11 on the southern half of the construction when

> I looked out the window to the north [and] saw a boilermaker on his knees, he had an airgun and he was tightening bolts in the middle of the span where boxes 4 and 5 joined. At this part of the

> bridge there was a buckle in the upper decking. The buckle was on the free edge of the northern section in the vicinity of boxes 4 and 5. I know that this buckle had been there for some time. I saw the buckle was getting worse and I also noticed flakes of rust flying off the steel decking where the buckle was. I think that what made me look out of the window was that I heard bolts snapping. When I saw what was happening, I said, 'We are going to go down.' By that I meant that I thought that the bridge was going to fall down. I sat on a box of bolts and waited for the bridge to fall. I cannot remember what happened after that because the bridge fell and I was knocked unconscious.

Rescue crews continued to toil frantically throughout the night and the following days, trying to extricate bodies from the mangled wreckage and save anyone still alive. The grisly scene was illuminated by floodlights.

As ever, there were too many heroes to honour, but the brave and selfless efforts of nine who pitched in with the rescue work that day would be officially recognised. Norman Lord, Deputy Chief Officer of the Port Emergency Service and Trevor Nixon, JHC's Southern Zone General Manager, each received an Order of the British Empire. Lord was cited for organising and coordinating most of the rescue services: 'In supervising the rescue of the injured and the recovery of the dead, [he], without regard for his own safety, displayed outstanding qualities of leadership as well as personal bravery of a high order.' Nixon was honoured for, despite having a leg encased in plaster, demonstrating 'outstanding qualities of leadership, organisation, motivation, persistence, courage and human concern'.

Seven others received a British Empire Medal. Elaine Armstrong, a nurse with the St John Ambulance Brigade, was praised for 'exceptional devotion in alleviating the pain and suffering of many victims. She worked without rest for eight hours and set a fine example to others in caring for casualties'. Donald Cook, Royston Kilford, Frederick Rowe, Barry Gorsuch, all divers with the Port Emergency Service, 'displayed personal bravery without regard for their own safety in searching the wreckage for long periods in hazardous conditions'. Another St John Ambulance staffer, Alan Sparks, 'worked tirelessly in a confined space for many hours, in great discomfort and at considerable personal risk, to extricate a casualty trapped under a mass of wreckage'. Gus Stromberg, a rigger employed by JHC, 'waded into slimy mud to rescue victims and worked through the afternoon and evening helping to retrieve the dead and injured.'

'Melbourne has experienced the bitter taste of grief,' wrote *Sydney Morning Herald* reporter James Cunningham, poignantly chronicling his on-the-scene impressions.

> Along the dark Yarra tonight, lights flash and twinkle from the ships and the wharves. Life and work goes on but with a sense of tragedy and loss. Out at the bridge the cranes sift through the heaps of debris swinging out their burdens of metal and rubble. Then the rescue workers go in probing in the hope and fear of finding another victim. Above them the massive 200 ft high supports of the bridge soar away into the darkness. This work will go on all night and tomorrow in eight-hour shifts. The spot where the bridge suddenly fell is an ugly and forbidding part of Melbourne. Mud flats are edged with thick stagnant water. A nearby chemical factory pours smoke and fumes over the river. Tonight at the West Gate Bridge the very air smells foul and dead.

The inevitable angry recriminations began on 16 October, even as the designers and builders canvassed ways to get construction underway again as early as possible. How could so terrible a disaster occur? Victorian Premier Sir Henry Bolte, who had turned the first sod when construction got underway in April 1968, announced that there would be a Royal Commission 'to establish all the facts – to find out who was at fault'.

The Royal Commission, headed by Mr Justice Barber, assisted by world-renowned engineers Professor Frank Bull and Sir Hubert Shirley-Smith, sat for the first time on 4 November 1970, at Hawthorn Town Hall. Present were witnesses, experts, senior executives of the design and construction firms, and fifty lawyers, including twelve Queen's Counsel. As testimony was heard and various contractors accused and denied, ducked and dived, seeking to avoid blame themselves while apportioning it to the others, the corpse of the collapsed span lay in the marshes of the Yarra's western bank, workers scampering over it like yellow-jacketed ants, dismantling and untangling the wreckage and taking it away with cranes and trucks.

In early January, the squabbling at the Royal Commission was put into tragic perspective. Frank Piermarini, the rigger who had ridden the section down into the river and lived to tell the tale, died. He became the thirty-fifth and last victim of the disaster. Since describing his ordeal and thanking God for sparing him, he had had three operations on his terrible injuries, but was claimed by a lung infection.

After eighty days in which the Commissioners heard fifty-two witnesses, pored over 319 exhibits and listened to three million words of evidence, the Royal Commission delivered its findings. Chief among them was that 'compression buckling' had caused the span to fall. Also, that the British designers of the West Gate Bridge, Freeman Fox and Partners, had failed to provide a 'proper and careful regard to the process of structural design', and had neglected to properly check the safety of construction proposals mooted by the original contractors, World Services and Constructions Pty Ltd (WSC). So, said Mr Justice Barber, 'the margins of safety for the bridge were inadequate during erection; they would also have been inadequate in the service condition had the bridge been completed.'

It would be wrong, the Commissioners agreed, to blame the bridge disaster on the sole act of removing the bolts on the day of the collapse. 'In our opinion the sources of the failure lie much further back; they arise from two main causes.' This was the Freeman Fox and Partners' failure, and also the 'unusual method' that had been put forward by WSC for the erection of spans 10 and 11 on the west side of the bridge and spans 14 and 15 on the east side.

> This erection method, if it was to be successful, required more than usual care on the part of the contractor and a consequential

> responsibility on the consultants to ensure that such care was indeed exercised. Neither of the contractors [WSC and JHC] appeared to have appreciated this need for great care.

Freeman Fox, ruled the inquiry, had not prevented WSC and JHC from using procedures that were liable to be dangerous.

JHC, which took over the construction of the bridge from WSC, was absolved from any responsibility for removing the bolts, which led directly to the collapse. The unbolting had been ordered and supervised by Freeman Fox engineer Jack Hindshaw and his more junior site engineers David Ward and Peter Crossley, who did not have 'any calculations to give a true insight into the danger of unbolting at the time ... If Hindshaw was really aware of the situation and if, as we believe, he did discuss the problem with Ward, then he should have instantly vetoed any suggestion of taking out the bolts.'

The Commission, however, did chastise JHC on a number of fronts. Its site engineers were too junior and inexperienced to be making decisions on such a major project as the West Gate Bridge. It had committed 'the gravest of errors' in suggesting that concrete blocks be placed on one side of the span to even up the misalignment. The company was also guilty of overconfidence and failing to seek advice from the staff of its predecessor WSC.

Summing up, Justice Barber called the West Gate Bridge collapse 'probably the most tragic industrial accident in the history of Victoria'.

Work duly recommenced on the West Gate Bridge in early 1972. It would resemble the original, ill-fated, bridge, but the deck of the new bridge would be different: the steel and concrete deck of the original design was replaced by a stiffened steel deck. The cost of building had soared from $42 million to over $200 million. Construction delays and industrial disputes slowed the building, and it wasn't until 15 November 1978 that the bridge was opened and cars streamed across the span.

A month before the official opening, on 15 October, a memorial plaque, paid for by the workers who subsequently completed the West Gate Bridge, was unveiled. The plaque's inscription reads:

Construction workers employed on West Gate Bridge erected and dedicated this memorial to their 35 workmates who were killed when a span of the bridge collapsed during construction at 11.50 a.m. on 15th October 1970. Our comrades who lost their lives were:

Royvin Barbuto, boilermaker; Ross Bigmore, carpenter; Amadeo Boscolo, carpenter; Bernard Butters, boilermaker; Cyril Carmichael, ironworker; Peter Crossley, engineer; Peter Dawson, rigger; Abraham Eden, rigger; Anthony Falzon, carpenter; Esequial Fernandez, ironworker; Bernard Fitzsimmons, ironworker; Victor Gerada, ironworker; John Grist, boilermaker; William Harburn, boilermaker; Jack Hindshaw, engineer; Trevor Hunsdale, fitter; John Little, rigger; Charles Lund, rigger; Peter McGuire, rigger; Ian Miller, engineer; Jeremiah Murphy, rigger; Dennis O'Brien, rigger; Joseph Ozelis, first aid; Frank Piermarini, rigger; George Pram, rigger; Lesley Scarlett, ironworker; Christopher Stewart, boilermaker; Alfonso Suarez, boilermaker; William Tracy, engineer; George Tsihilidis, boilermaker; Edgar Upsdell, ironworker; Robert West, boilermaker; Robert Whelan, boilermaker; Patrick Woods, rigger; Barry Wright, boilermaker.

IN MEMORY OF WORKERS OF ALL LANDS WHO ARE KILLED IN INDUSTRIAL ACCIDENTS.

Today the West Gate Bridge is an essential link between the west of Melbourne and its environs and the city. Still, few of those who remember the events of 15 October 1970 can cross the bridge high over the Yarra without a shudder.

CHAPTER 12

CYCLONE TRACY

25 DECEMBER 1974

In Australia's history, there have been more ferocious cyclones, but Cyclone Tracy is the only one ever to lay waste to an entire capital city.

Christmas morning, 1974: while Australians were waking to pleasant thoughts of the presents and feasting to come, Darwin and its inhabitants were being assailed by a tempest that would kill a total of seventy-one, flatten the city (scarcely a building escaped total destruction or severe damage), and turn its citizens into homeless refugees.

Cyclone Tracy first came to the notice of the Australian Bureau of Meteorology on 20 December as a depression in the Arafura Sea. The weather watchers tracked it as it slowly moved south-west, intensifying all the time, and passed by Cape Fourcroy, on the western tip of Bathurst Island, on 23 and 24 December. It was a formidable storm, but there seemed no cause for alarm, until late on Christmas Eve the cyclone – for this is what it had now become – turned sharply east-south-east and headed straight for Darwin.

On the afternoon of Christmas Eve, an eerie, troubling calm descended on the city, born of low and heavy cloud, intense humidity, squalling rain and keening winds. This, however, did not deter the Christmas parties which were in full swing that day. Darwin's saviour, Major-General Alan Stretton, captured the mood of Darwin on Christmas Eve when he quoted a newspaperman in his book *The Furious Days*: 'Pubs were full of cheerful people discussing the cyclone forecasts. They were laughing and joking, even singing how cyclones never hit Darwin.'

Other Darwinites took the situation more seriously and hoped against hope that the mighty storm would change course – as storms had in the past – and spare them. Their prayers went unanswered.

Cyclone Tracy struck Darwin at 1 a.m. on 25 December. The eye passed over the city around 4 a.m. Though small as tropical cyclones go – Tracy's radius was only around 50 kilometres – it was extraordinarily powerful, and because it was slow-moving, its winds had ample time to create maximum havoc over four terrible hours, until it passed over Darwin and rumbled on to Arnhem Land. Before it was obliterated, the anemometer at Darwin Airport recorded a wind gust of 217 kilometres per hour (though many who lived through them swear that the winds reached 280 kilometres per hour at their peak). The damage done to Darwin by Tracy was increased by the inadequate construction of many houses.

In the last hours of 24 December, when weather authorities realised that Cyclone Tracy was bound for Darwin, then a city of 48 000 people, warnings were issued. Advised the RAAF Cyclone Operations Bureau: '277 degrees. 17 miles. Leading Edge 3½ miles Charles Point. Indications are will deflect across Charles Point to Darwin.'

A Bureau of Meteorology broadcast stated that 'Cyclone Tracy has destructive winds of up to 120 kilometres per hour and these are expected to hit the Darwin area tonight and tomorrow'.

But the warnings went largely unheard. With most people by now asleep or preoccupied with tomorrow's festivities, few Darwinites were listening. The first many of the sleeping knew of Tracy was a loud roar which many likened to that of a jet plane or a speeding train, and then the smashing and pounding as their homes were dismantled and came crashing down. Cars, boats and anything else not nailed or tied down were flung high into the air. The areas that suffered worst were the coastal suburbs of Rapid Creek, Nightcliff and Fannie Bay. Six prisoners took their chance to escape from the Fannie Bay Jail, which was demolished.

In the coming days, people told of their experiences: 'The top of the house just went *pow*! Then there was nothing left'; 'The roof went first, then the walls. We just got out in time before everything went'; 'We lost everything. Our clothing, our crockery – the lot'; 'I saw a Volkswagen car that had been picked up by the cyclone and deposited on the roof of a two-storey building. Even today I can scarcely believe it.'

The suddenness and totality of the destruction were hard for survivors to comprehend. Said one:

> The roof was torn off our house with a ... roar. Seconds later the walls were peeled off the four sides of the building, leaving us shocked and exposed to the cyclone. I grabbed one of the children by the leg as the gale looked like blowing her away into the darkness.

> My husband, my mother, myself and our two children retreated into the bathroom. I climbed into the bath with the children while mother and my husband huddled under the hand basin. By this time, the walls of the bathroom had gone and we were virtually hanging onto the fittings. When the wind subsided a little we made a dash for shelter under the house wreckage.

And another:

> It was as though our home was being shaken by a giant. I was waiting for us to become airborne at any moment. The miracle of Tracy is that there were not thousands killed. Many people did die, but the city was so completely destroyed it is a mystery how the majority survived.

Some described the temporary lull as the eye of the cyclone passed over:

> There were furious winds and then when the eye passed over, nothing. The lull, in which there was not a breath of wind or rain, lasted 20 minutes. Then the wind began to build again and I heard it ripping the tin from the roof of my home.

Small details stuck in some survivors' minds:

> It was still raining, teeming, though the wind had abated. Hardly anything was left standing. All our 15ft high mahogany trees were uprooted, lying about the yard and over the broken fences. Everywhere there was corrugated iron. Our fridge had been tossed like a toy halfway across the yard. Our car had been swivelled right around. We'd had wallpaper with pretty flowers on it on our kitchen wall. Bits of the wall with the flowers were scattered all over our neighbour's fence. That's what hit me the most … the flowers on our kitchen wall.

Darwin Hospital and twenty specially established first aid centres were overwhelmed by patients suffering broken bones and cuts caused by flying glass, iron and assorted debris, and falls.

Parliament was recalled, and acting Prime Minister Dr Jim Cairns, red-eyed and haggard on his return to Canberra from the ruins of Darwin, was typically eloquent.

> Darwin represents so much to Australia that it will have to be rebuilt, but I can't say yet whether it will be on the present site. What happened in Darwin on Christmas morning has never happened in Australia before. Darwin is devastated. Darwin is destroyed. There is virtually no building in Darwin that is not seriously damaged. Darwin looks like a battlefield or Hiroshima. The people have been magnificent and their morale is high. It was an honour yesterday to move often silently among them and try to share a little in their tragedy and their courage. The loss of Darwin is a national loss. Its cost must and will be shared by the Australian people. A plan is emerging to safeguard the health of those in Darwin and for the rebuilding of the city, which will take time and come later.

Dr Cairns had met with Opposition Leader Bill Snedden, who agreed to work in a bipartisan manner with the government to reconstruct the flattened city.

Continued Cairns:

> The Government and the Opposition must join together in this matter. There will be failures and mistakes, but critics can be constructive and will always be needed. Most of the people of Darwin have lost their homes – often the result of a lifetime's work – and none is able to do more than search in the wreckage, moved by some hope of finding something of value, some link with yesterday. Some work feverishly, some with calm application, and some have not yet emerged from their shock.

When dawn broke and shaken residents stumbled out from under their beds or from their bathrooms (deemed the safest room in most homes) into the daylight, they realised that they were residents of a destroyed city. 'There was nothing out there,' said one Darwinite. 'It looked like a bomb had hit.' Mourned another, 'The heart of Darwin has been ripped out.'

The residents' horror was shared by the rest of the nation as word got out during Christmas Day, despite Darwin's ruined telephone, telegraph and telex systems. The city was declared a disaster area and Australia's emergency and defence forces were marshalled and sent there to mop up, recover the dead from the rubble and evacuate the living. The National Disasters Organisation and the Red Cross rushed clothing, blankets, food and medical supplies to Darwin, as well as doctors and nurses to tend the hundreds of injured. Construction workers flew to Darwin to help rebuild homes and repair damaged water and power lines.

Amid fears of disease, volunteers were designated to collect garbage from the streets, already rotting and verminous in the high summer heat. Stray cats and dogs were shot.

Prime Minister Gough Whitlam, declaring himself 'horrified by the appalling loss of life and the destruction', returned immediately to Australia from his trip to Sicily, Malta and Crete. He walked the battered streets of Darwin with residents and visited the city's schools, those that were still standing having been turned into refuges for the homeless. As the Minister for the Northern Territory, Dr Rex Patterson, said, 'People are huddled everywhere. They are in schools. Thousands in schools ... Little children in schools.'

By Boxing Day, Australia and the world knew a calamity of terrible proportions had befallen Darwin. As well as the death toll (on 26 December it was put at forty-four, but it would rise) and the homelessness arising from the destruction of homes and buildings, an unknown number of ships had been sunk and RAAF and commercial planes destroyed. 'I flew over Hiroshima,' said Group Captain David Hitchins, commander of the RAAF base at Darwin, 'and Darwin looks just like it.'

Everywhere trees and power poles had been uprooted or snapped clean off. There was no electricity or sewerage (trench latrines were dug with front-end loaders and backhoes), no fresh water or food. Major-General Stretton, Director-General of the National Disasters Organisation, announced that details were still fairly sketchy, but spoke of cars being piled against telephone poles, grief-stricken and traumatised people wandering the streets, and of an 8-storey building which 'literally did the tango'. He arrived in Darwin airport late on Christmas night and met immediately with the Commissioner of Police, the Director of Emergency Services, the Secretary of the Department of the Northern Territory and the Minister for the Northern Territory to devise a strategy to effectively and cool-headedly coordinate disaster relief operations. Stretton, who, like his colleagues, would barely sleep for the next week, later labelled 25 December 1974, as 'one hell of a Christmas Day'.

In a poignant – and prescient – Boxing Day editorial, the *Sydney Morning Herald* attempted to come to terms with the disaster.

> We in Australia expect Christmas Day to be a happy time for most of us; and so no doubt it was, for most of us ... But for one Australian city Christmas Day brought terror and tragedy. The extent of the death and injuries and the damage caused early on Christmas Day by the cyclone which struck Darwin with such terrible velocity may not be known for days. It is certain that it is very extensive: we have on our hands probably the worst natural disaster to have afflicted an Australian city.
>
> There are at least 40 dead. Hundreds are injured. About 90 per cent of the city has been wrecked or badly damaged. A great number of the population (about 40 000) are homeless. Some 20 000 may be without food or clothing. The city is without fundamental amenities, such as power and communications. The loss in money terms can hardly begin to be estimated. Australians, it can be said with confidence, will respond in two ways. There will be everywhere profound, but also practical, sympathy for the sufferers; already last night authorities in the south were receiving many offers of help or enquiries about how to help.
>
> The more important immediate response depends on the

> capacity of the nation to mount a swift rescue operation and to rush aid to the devastated area. The difficulties involved in this immense challenge are great because of the remoteness of the area. The new National Emergency Operations Centre, opened in Canberra only in October, faces a test of unimagined magnitude. It will be astonishing if it is yet equipped to meet it. The great burden will fall on existing State emergency organisations and, above all, on the Armed Services. Most of us at this stage can do little but sympathise, but our chance to help will come soon enough. No matter how large Canberra's aid will be – and it seems likely the bill will be huge – there is bound to be a need for other funds to which cities, communities, organisations and individuals can contribute.

Australia heard the call to arms and responded to the stricken city's need. There were moving scenes across the nation as people gathered to offer what aid they could. At the Salvation Army headquarters in Sydney, people queued for hours to give clothing, tinned food and cash. A boy donated his entire stash of Christmas presents and a man named Robert Horan gave his car, a Ford Falcon station wagon, handing over the keys to the Salvation Army officer with the words, 'Darwin needs it more than I.' Brigadier Geddes sat in the foyer, writing receipts and blessing the generous. As well as the Salvos, the St Vincent de Paul Society, CHUMS (Care and Help for Unmarried Mothers) and the Smith Family, the federal and state governments, newspapers and television and radio stations, church and community organisations and sporting clubs, trade unions and the Lord Mayors of all capital cities and towns established charity funds. The RSPCA sent inspectors to handle animals affected by Tracy.

By 27 December, with the cyclone still lingering in a now-weakened state over Arnhem Land, limited communication had been re-established, and RAAF, Qantas, TAA and Ansett planes, as well as the aircraft of corporations such as BHP, Comalco and Conzinc Riotinto, were delivering emergency personnel and supplies to Darwin, and evacuating the most seriously injured. Six Royal Australian Navy ships, including the aircraft carrier HMAS *Melbourne*, sped to the city.

Money was pledged by the governments of the United States and Great Britain, and Queen Elizabeth sent the following message:

> I am much distressed to learn of the tragic loss of life and damage caused by the cyclone which struck Darwin on Christmas Day. Prince Philip joins me in sending our deep sympathy to all those who have been bereaved and who have been made homeless.

Pope Paul VI bestowed 'God's comforting blessing' upon Darwin.

One of the most pressing tasks that fell to Major-General Stretton was the evacuation of more than 20 000 residents, in planes, ships and cars. (The final figure, it transpired, was over 30 000.) Said Stretton on 27 December:

> Anyone who is ill, pregnant women, babies and children will be going first. They will be flown to relatives if they have them in other states. If not, they will go into shelters that we are setting up in the capital cities. Apart from airlifts, there will be further evacuations when Navy ships arrive next week. Bread winners in general are expected to stay behind.

That day, some 2500 women and children were flown out. Residents were allowed to take pets with them. Government grants were made available, to tide over the dispossessed. It was early 1978 before Darwin regained the population level it had on Christmas Day, 1974 ... although some 60 per cent were post-Tracy newcomers. Today, time in Darwin is measured in terms of 'pre-Tracy' and 'post-Tracy'. Those who endured the cyclone and have remained are known by many in Darwin as 'true Darwinites', while those who came later are 'transients'.

With the lack of electricity plunging the city at night into pitch blackness, and so few inhabitants left in what was now a wasteland, police feared that Darwin was ripe for the picking by looters, and their fears were justified. The unattended possessions of victims, including cars, tyres and petrol, boats, televisions and radios and household goods, were stolen. In the first days after the cyclone, eleven men and two women were arrested and charged with being in unlawful possession of goods. Others who behaved shamefully when so many were covering themselves with glory were two Sydney men who went door-to-door with bogus identification claiming to be collecting for Darwin and keeping the money they extracted from good-hearted people for themselves. Another pair stole from an office $11 000 that was earmarked to aid Aboriginal missions. There were also allegations that local police and a small number of the 350-odd officers sent to Darwin from other forces to maintain order were themselves guilty of assault and theft, as well as being drunk in uniform. Later, when Darwin was being rebuilt, some bricklayers and carpenters were exposed for charging desperate home owners exorbitant fees for their reconstruction work, and some businesses callously cashed in on supply shortages.

On 28 December, the death toll of sixty-five was confirmed. That day, the *Sydney Morning Herald* editorialised once more:

> ... even with the extensive coverage given it by the press, radio and television, the magnitude of Darwin's tragedy is still difficult to grasp. Some 50 [sic] people are known to have died and more are missing; hundreds have been injured; thousands are homeless. A major city has been devastated and will have to be rebuilt ... at a cost estimated at $250 million. To that must be added the cost of relief work, particularly the evacuation of at least a quarter, perhaps a half, of Darwin's population. Yet who will count the cost today? Statistics merely indicate the immensity of the disaster. They say nothing of the physical or psychological suffering being endured by those who survived, nor of the bravery of individuals, such as Darwin's meteorological staff, who stayed at their posts until their equipment was blasted away by the wind.

As the new year loomed, authorities were able to report that there had been no outbreaks of disease (incidences of cholera, tetanus and typhoid were particularly feared) and that food stocks were mounting and water supplies improving. Also arriving were containers of shelter materials, and electrical and water purification gear. The Australian and English cricket teams, in the midst of an Ashes series, and tennis champions contesting the Australian Open, gave donations and prize money to the suffering of Darwin. The Australian and English cricketers moved among the crowd at the Boxing Day test match at the Melbourne Cricket Ground collecting donations from spectators in buckets and blankets.

It was announced that a glittering concert in aid of Darwin would be staged at the Opera House in early January. It was hoped that the show – which would star, among others, Dame Joan Sutherland, Rolf Harris, Helen Reddy, Barry Humphries, Dame Joan Hammond, Barry Crocker, Roger Woodward, Tommy Tycho and his orchestra, Donald Smith, Johnny Farnham, Graham Kennedy, David Frost and Kamahl – would raise $100 000. To this end, a handful of premium tickets priced from $1000 to $1 million were offered to the wealthy, while the balance sold for $10 each. When the tickets went on sale, they were snapped up by people who had been queuing all night to buy them. The two $1 million tickets and ten $10 000 tickets, however, went unsold. The concert was ecstatically received and the acclaimed classical pianist Roger Woodward published an open letter to those who attended.

> The support given by the people of Sydney for the Sydney Opera House Concert for Darwin last Saturday was nothing short of magnificent. I would like to thank the people of Sydney for their most generous response, together with all my colleagues and friends. All proceeds have gone to the Mayor of Darwin. I fly back to [my commitments in] Europe today, the very proud holder of an Australian passport.

Performers led by rock star Johnny O'Keefe travelled to Darwin and played a concert at Darwin High School. Half of the current population of the city showed up. The stars performed free and their transport to Darwin from the southern capitals was provided by TAA. The only difficulty was finding a piano for Jade Hurley to play that had not been splintered by Tracy. Happily, one reasonably intact piano was located on the roofless top floor of a building and manhandled to the venue in time.

On his walk through the ravaged streets of Darwin, Prime Minister Whitlam assured locals that the city would be rebuilt and restored and the people rehabilitated. The scenes he saw, he said, reminded him of when Darwin was bombed by the Japanese in 1942. 'People living here now live in no better conditions than they did during the war. I suppose 90 per cent of the buildings in Darwin have been built since the last cyclone in 1947. It's clear that the method of construction was not suitable for people living in a cyclone belt.'

Shortly after, the Prime Minister announced the formation of the federal government's Darwin Reconstruction Commission to plan and coordinate the rebuilding of the city. The new Darwin would spring from the site of the old one, and he expected the job to take at least five years and cost $600 million. The Commission would comprise captains of industry as well as representatives of the federal Departments of the Northern Territory, Housing and Construction and Urban and Regional Development, as well as officials chosen by the Northern Territory Legislative Assembly and Darwin City Council.

The first priority would be to implement building codes that would ensure that the new buildings would withstand a cyclone. Suggestions that would be incorporated into Darwin building codes included the recommended (though not compulsory) construction of a core within each new house strong enough to withstand flying debris, which could be used as a cyclone shelter; smaller windows and stronger window frames; the use of roof battens tying the roof to the foundations; and bolts and cyclone ties to hold the house together even in winds of up to 240 kilometres per hour. Darwinites would be repatriated to their city as soon as there was somewhere for them to live and work.

At least $58 million would be paid by the federal government to compensate those who lost homes and businesses. Over $6 million was donated to the Darwin Cyclone Tracy Relief Fund. Insurance companies faced a $220 million payout.

Meanwhile, there was the grisly task of identifying the bodies of those killed in the cyclone on land and on sea. Among the deceased were thirteen children aged under 12. Police officers had their work cut out, because only about ten of the bodies carried identification. They were photographed and the photos, along with details of clothing and distinguishing marks, were sent to police stations in Darwin and police headquarters in every state in case anyone came seeking information about a missing loved one.

There was widespread dismay from the Darwinites who remained behind when Major-General Stretton – mindful of heightened emotions in the city and the hard work to be done – decreed that no alcohol be consumed on New Year's Eve. The people of Darwin were grateful to Stretton, and admired him enormously for all that he had done for them, but there was no chance, in this case, of his orders being followed.

On 31 December, Major-General Alan Stretton – 'Darwin's Churchill', as some were now calling him – handed over the city to civilian control. In June 1975 he would be appointed an Officer of the Order of Australia for 'eminent services in duties of great responsibility', and he was joint Australian of the Year for 1975.

In taking his leave, Stretton made a broadcast to the people of Darwin:

> It would be wrong of me, now that I judge my job as over, to stay on here. There is nobody in Darwin, from the highest to the lowest in the land, who has not been magnificent. I am no longer wanted here. I just came in and did a pretty simple task given to me by the Acting Prime Minister. I feel my duty is to get back home ... I can't really say how I feel. But to those who have shared with me, I thank you from the bottom of my heart. I feel it would be improper to steal the glory that belongs to you all. Thank you. I will be back. I want to make sure that the bloody garbage is cleared up and there is no sign of a cyclone in this town. Otherwise I'll be asking a few questions. God bless you all.

CHAPTER 13

THE GRANVILLE TRAIN SMASH

18 JANUARY 1977

For veteran train driver Edward Olencewicz and the passengers who boarded his early morning express bound for Parramatta and the city of Sydney, most of them commuting to work, Tuesday, 18 January 1977 dawned a work day like any other. But the journey ended in horror, injury and death. Near Granville railway station, the train derailed and struck the supporting pillars of an overhead bridge, bringing the bridge crashing down on the third and fourth carriages of the eight-carriage train. Some eighty-three passengers were killed and more than 200 were injured.

The train ride to disaster began, right on time, at 6.09 a.m. that muggy, rainy morning, when the train departed Mount Victoria in the Blue Mountains, about 90 kilometres west of Sydney, with just a handful of people on board. Station by station, the train filled up. Some fifty commuters boarded at Katoomba, and 500 or so joined the train as it made its way down the mountain. By the time it departed Blacktown station, there was standing room only. It was 8.12 when the train approached Granville station, travelling less than the permitted speed limit of 80 kilometres per hour.

As the track curved to the left, the train jumped it to the right, smashing into eight steel stanchions that supported the upper decking of the Bold Street overhead bridge. The train overturned, slid more than 60 metres and came to a literal grinding halt. A few seconds later the 250-tonne northern span of the bridge collapsed onto the train, along with the northern end of the centre span, crushing the third and fourth carriages where the sardined commuters had been chatting, reading newspapers and books, or lost in thought. Reported one eyewitness, 'The train gave a shudder and jumped across the tracks then it hit that bridge and there was this terrible thunder as the bridge went down.'

On seeing the bridge fall onto the train, a member of the public named Jack McKeown, who ironically happened to have once been an engine driver, ran to a public phone and called the emergency number 000: 'Give me the ambulance,' he cried. 'There's been a huge train crash!' Police cars and wagons, fire engines, ambulances with sirens squealing, doctors, nurses, all available police and the Police Rescue Squad were rushed to

Granville. Fifteen cranes (some of 125-tonne capacity) arrived, along with jackhammers, tractors, oxyacetylene torches, drills, picks, crowbars, sledgehammers, ropes, steel cables and other rescue equipment. Reporters and priests were at the site, doing, under dreadful pressure, what they had been trained to do. Some 1500 members of the public, including frantic family and friends of passengers, flocked to the scene of carnage and had to be forcibly kept clear by police.

Down on the track, those passengers who were unscathed or only slightly injured scrambled from their carriages and did their best to comfort the more injured and maimed until the professionals could reach them. Driver Olencewicz when rescued from his overturned cabin compartment wept, 'I don't know how it happened. I can't understand it. It all happened so quickly.' He was heavily sedated and taken to hospital in an ambulance.

The Salvation Army arrived within a half hour or so, laden with food and drink. By the time the rescue operation was over they had served four and a half thousand meals, and gallons of tea, coffee, cordial and soft drinks. Local snack bars and restaurant proprietors brought meals as well. Said badly shaken Salvation Army officer and boxer Trevor King to a reporter:

> I've been around. I was a professional fighter and I'm used to blood and gore. I've been called out by the police to accidents where you need a crowbar to get people out, but I've never seen anything like this. It was so horrifying I couldn't even have imagined it was possible. You just couldn't recognise [the victims]. I've been offering moral support, liaising with the police and going down where the men are working and talking to them. I know when a man comes to the limit of his endurance. I've seen that before. Now I've seen men pass that point and go on with new reserves of strength.

Hospitals all over Sydney were warned to prepare to be overwhelmed with victims of the crash (some ninety-two people would be treated in hospitals). People queued at blood banks to give blood – 1600 donors would give for the cause.

With enormous difficulty, and using crowbars and oxyacetylene torches, the Police Rescue Squad entered the crushed and tangled carriages – dark, airless hell-holes – to rescue survivors, often with their bare hands. There was no overt emotion, just grim determination. Doctors were on the heels of the rescuers to treat those in pain and give plasma. Said one doctor as he stumbled out of carriage three for a brief and desperately needed break: 'We have to forget about the dead. I have seen so many trapped and dead, but I cannot help them. We must concentrate on saving those who can be saved.'

Now began the task of breaking up and lifting the portions of concrete slab from carriages three and four. At 11.35 the rescuers were hastily evacuated when, with a terrifying rumble, the bridge began to shift. It settled and the rescuers returned.

By 1.10, the first bodies were carried from the wreckage. Work continued all night, the site eerily lit by arc lights. The removal of the bodies and the concrete slab continued for days, as did work to repair the tracks and re-establish the train service. Of the seventy-three occupants in carriage one, which overturned and slid out of the range of the falling bridge, eight died; nobody perished in carriage two; there were forty-four fatalities among the seventy-seven occupants of carriage three; and thirty-one of the sixty-four passengers in carriage four died. Carriages five, six, seven and eight were unscathed.

The last body was removed around 3.15 p.m. on 19 January.

A red-eyed Father Kevin McGovern many times that day was called to administer the last rites to victims. 'It's terrible under that bridge,' he told a gaggle of reporters. 'The carriage is flat. You can see arms and legs sticking out.' A fellow priest, Father Michael Campion, despaired: 'They had a bridge on top of them. They could not move. There wasn't any impression of life down there.' Volunteer rescuer Stephen Dawson reported that 'People were crushed. A lot of them had missing limbs. One man had his head severed. Inside there it looked like all these people had been sitting reading newspapers because of the way their arms were cut. They were still just sitting there.' The man who led the rescue, Sergeant Joe Beecroft, who toiled for eight hours without a break, mourned, 'This is the worst job I have ever had. Sometimes we were working in space a foot high.'

Reporter James Cunningham of the *Sydney Morning Herald* was another to rise to the occasion that day. He wrote evocatively of the rescue operation:

> The small victories of this day of horror in the suburbs were the rescue of those still alive after the catastrophe. I watched them carried out. First there was a woman in a tattered green dress, her face covered in an oxygen mask. Then came a girl, young and fair, but covered in grey dust. She looked beyond hope. But she was still alive and the doctors and the nurses worked on her. And she moved. And an ambulance rushed her away shrilling its song of disaster ... So the battle went on. Men burrowed into wreckage like blue-overalled moles. Stretcher bearers carried their burdens along the line and up the grassy slopes to where the ambulances were waiting. The living were greeted with relief and hope and smooth efficiency by doctors and nurses whose overalls were now stained with blood. The dead passed quietly, covered in blankets. Their exposed footwear told us something about them: a pair of heavy boots meant perhaps a labourer; a pair of polished shoes an office worker.

As Dr Ernest Pedersen, Senior Medical Officer of the NSW Police Department, who was early to the scene, later told the Judicial Inquiry into the disaster:

> In those carriages there was a scene of carnage that almost defies description. Most of the passengers were dead, and it is my opinion that for most of them death was quick and suffering minimal. However, scattered among the dead were a few passengers who remained alive and it was a long and tedious task [for rescuers] to get to these people. Gas had been detected in the wrecked carriages and there was a very real danger of a further collapse of the bridge.

There were many heroes that day. Constable John Wilson continued rescue work long into the day despite injuring his back when rubble fell on him. Police Rescue Squad member Constable Richard Lamb was driving near Granville when he heard a newsflash on the radio. He called squad headquarters and requested that as many rescuers and as much equipment as possible be despatched to Granville. Arriving at the accident site, he saw that a rescue unit was already there. He helped himself to a chainsaw and accompanied Constable Bruce Game to the carriage that had suffered the most damage, carriage three.

He told the inquiry:

> At the front of the carriage I saw a number of people lying among the seats. The roof of the train had collapsed on top of them and there was a space of about 6 or 7 feet from the front door to where the roof had collapsed. I released a man and a woman by lifting a part of the roof then I cut access into the carriage with a chainsaw and freed a further four or five people.

Constable Lamb told the inquiry that he could hear the trapped screaming and calling out for help. Police Rescue Squad members led by Sergeant Joe Beecroft had appeared in the carriage at 8.40, recalled Lamb. 'For the next hour we worked removing the injured until we came to the concrete slab of the bridge which had crushed the carriage.' There, he said, 'I looked further into the carriage with a torch and I could see movement behind a deceased [woman] who was lying in the aisle.' It was a badly injured woman who Lamb could see moving. 'I could see she was still alive, but she was lying in a pool of blood and brain matter.' He and other rescuers formed a human chain and combined to drag the woman clear.

Constable Lamb was then directed to the other end of the carriage to help free an injured man who was trapped by his legs and had suffered serious injuries to the lower half of his body. Because the man, who was receiving a blood transfusion, was wedged in by the bodies of deceased victims, a hydraulic spreader was used to pull him free. After then assisting in the rescue of a girl, Lamb spent the rest of that day and the next removing bodies from under the concrete slab after it had been broken up.

Sergeant Joe Beecroft was an inspiration to the survivors, and to the men in his squad. He threw himself into his terrible task. He issued an edict to his rescuers that once they were with their 'patient' they could not leave him or her until they were pulled from the wreckage. 'Maybe they're lying in darkness,' he told a reporter from the *Australian Women's Weekly* on the day. 'I always give them my hand. That's what people want – to feel someone else is there. To touch your hand. They've been very calm, very good. One man told me, "If I'm going to die, I'm not going to die alone."'

At the Judicial Inquiry he recalled how among the first sights to greet him had been three dead people partially buried by concrete.

> I had seen many dead people over the years and it was obvious from these people's severe head injuries that there was no possibility of them being alive. I heard a man calling for help from about the centre of the carriage and with the help of other rescuers I started work to reach him. This operation was suspended for a short time while a doctor amputated the arm of a dead woman so we could get further under the carriage. The man was in a satisfactory condition although a seat frame was jammed into his groin.

Once the man was freed and taken out, Beecroft and his men moved further into the death carriage. Among the littered bodies he saw a woman who, while buried beneath rubble, was still alive. 'To free her we had to cut away the roof of the carriage and steel electrical cable support. The roof of the carriage in the area was crushed by the weight of the concrete to within 20 inches of the floor.'

Heroism was not confined to the rescuers. At around 6 p.m., the squad brought the battered form of victim Bryan Gordon from the wreckage. Gordon, 31, of Emu Plains, was the last of the living to be extricated. He was cut from the concrete in a 10-hour operation during which he remained conscious. Said Beecroft at the inquiry:

> Constable Game comforted him the whole time. Bryan Gordon remained calm during the whole of the operation and was most considerate of other persons. He was aware of the situation he was in and the injuries he had sustained, realising he had no hope of survival. On a number of occasions he told us to assist [other] persons who were trapped and for whom something could be done. During this time, a large portion of the bridge parapet was hanging over Mr Gordon's head. It could have fallen, crushing him and the police and ambulance officers who remained with him.

Bryan Gordon, despite the work of his rescuers and his own valiant spirit, would later die in hospital.

Sergeant Beecroft also ordered that it was to be a priority of those lifting the slabs with cranes and breaking up the concrete that care be taken so that further mutilation of bodies be reduced. He lauded the work 'of the gang of men who worked tirelessly operating the jackhammers breaking up the bridge, the skill of the crane drivers and their crews'.

Inevitably, in the days after the crash incredible stories of luck and tragedy emerged. Fashion designer Jenny Kee regularly commuted from her home in Blackheath to her premises in Sydney's Strand Arcade in the third carriage of the 6.09 to Sydney – for some reason it was her favourite – but on 18 January she had the good fortune to arrive late at Blackheath station, and the stationmaster instructed her and her 22-month-old daughter Grace to enter the first carriage. She would suffer shock and Grace a small head cut. 'I've always had energy for living and Granville made that much more intense for me,' Kee later reflected. Commuter Bill Linney, standing in the aisle in the middle of carriage three, was knocked from his feet by the impact when the train hit the first stanchion but in the few seconds before the bridge fell he instinctively scrambled to another – as it transpired, safer – part of the carriage. John Stewart was sitting in the doomed fourth carriage, but went to the toilet in a carriage further back just before the crash, and so survived. Tragically, five young employees of the ANZ Bank perished. The Watts family of Penrith had two sons on the train, travelling in different carriages; Michael, 11, survived, but his brother David, 25, did not. David Watts was identified by the watch he wore, which was inscribed to him with love by his wife Clare. One of the deceased, William Gemmell of Lawson, was father to nine children aged from 18 months to 19 years.

The residents of Toowoomba in Queensland offered to host holidays in their homes for loved ones of the dead, and the folk of Darwin, still rebuilding their city after Cyclone Tracy in 1974, set up a fund to help the Granville victims.

Rescuer Ken Howard would write beautifully of seeing

> an elderly couple [lying in the wrecked carriage] peacefully embraced. I thought that they obviously knew they were going to die in that packed train. After it hit the pylon, tipped over and split in two, they must have heard the bridge-slab creaking [and] about to drop due to lack of support. Did they tell each other of their undying love? I think they did. I could see they loved each other. Their arms had to be broken to break their embrace.

Vivian Stewart, an unemployed factory hand, was a passenger in the third carriage who remained at the scene after the crash, helping rescuers all night and the next day. No one would have blamed him had he cried off. He had seen terrible things. He was in the toilet when the bridge fell on the train

> and I opened the door of the toilet and I saw the concrete lying on the top of the back of my carriage, and it was all crushed down. I saw a man sitting in the second seat from the front on the left side of the train. He was bald-headed and his head was in his lap, and the concrete was on his back. He was gasping and blue in the face. I tried to pull him out by the arms, but I couldn't move him. On the right side of the train I saw a pair of women's legs sticking out from under the concrete and a man's leg and arm who had been sitting next to her ... I could hear a lady crying from under the concrete somewhere and then some moans and groans.

Jim Fisher, 33, of Mount Riverview was much-mourned. He was a family man and a pillar of his community who until recently had been a volunteer fighting bushfires in the Blue Mountains. He was known for growing extraordinarily beautiful native flowers in his garden and for his love of the bush. Said a friend:

> He helped build our community – he was a real keystone. He was one of the most unassuming and generous people. He went back to work from holidays on Monday and bought a quarterly ticket for $80. The next day he was dead. His death and those of the others is a real tragedy. Everyone around here knows two or three people who were killed at Granville.

When Jim Fisher was buried, his coffin was festooned with yellow, pink and red wildflowers.

Psychiatrists warned that the bereaved should not try to constrain their grief or resort to medication to ease the emotional pain; they should cry and air their sorrow. Repressing their intense feelings could lead to psychological problems later. The many church services held to remember the Granville victims – including the one at Sydney's St Mary's Cathedral, which 4500 attended – were packed with mourners.

In an ugly development, when Edward Olencewicz was released from hospital, he and his wife received a number of abusive phone calls from people blaming him. Police organised for all calls to the Olencewicz home to be screened. The train driver, who had an unblemished record and was well-liked by his colleagues, was shattered. Later, he would be described by the train's guard, Leslie Thomas, as a much-respected train driver and 'one of those drivers that no matter what sort of a train you put in front of him he will give you a smooth ride and smooth stop.'

The Judicial Inquiry, which began in February, was headed by Judge Staunton, Chief Judge of the NSW District Court, assisted by two independent technical assessors. New South Wales Premier Neville Wran, in announcing the inquiry, said it would have wide powers of investigation into the causes and circumstances of the accident and be empowered to make observations on aspects of railway safety. The Premier said he hoped it would expose the deficiencies of the state's rail system.

One of the first witnesses called was Edward Olencewicz, who told the inquiry that on the journey on 18 January, 'everything had gone perfectly'. When his train left Parramatta station it was running just a minute behind schedule, and travelling at 78 kilometres per hour, and then he shut the throttle to reduce the speed to 20 kilometres per hour to accommodate a restriction at upcoming Clyde station. Approaching Granville station, Olencewicz had heard a loud 'crack' and at that moment

> the engine dropped off the rails onto the sleepers. The engine started to rock and roll sideways and upwards and was heading towards the stanchions. We hit the bridge ... The front of the engine hit the first stanchion and then it went through, taking all the stanchions in front of it. It went right along the foundations which support the stanchions.

The engine had rolled onto its right side and slid along for a distance of one and a half engine lengths before stopping. Olencewicz was pinned in the cabin.

Other passengers told the inquiry that they had felt bumps and heard cracks on the track just before the accident. Ivan Turner of Penrith, who was sitting in the first carriage, described 'a bang and we started to bounce up and down ... and the carriage started tilting and the side I was on started to go down. The right side of the carriage went up into the air and a girl about 11 was catapulted from her seat across me and I grabbed her as she would have gone out the window.' When pressed by Judge Staunton, Turner said the bang he heard was 'a metallic grinding noise ... similar to a sledgehammer striking an anvil.'

After hearing from passengers, witnesses and experts, Judge Staunton released his findings 31 May 1977. He blamed the derailment which brought the bridge down on the unsatisfactory condition of parts of the track and held poor railway track maintenance by the Public Transport Commission responsible. 'Inadequacies of policy, training, supervision and application had developed in the track maintenance system.' The Public Transport Commission, he found, had failed to detect the faults and remedy them. 'It was almost inevitable that a derailment would occur so long as the poor condition of the track remained uncorrected.' Some parts of the track were wider than allowed, the rails were not stable but moved sideways and their original curve had altered with time. One of the rails was badly worn in two places, as were the spikes that anchored it. Urgent changes had to be made to training and communications within the Public Transport Commission.

The inquiry also found that the span of the Bold Street bridge which collapsed on the carriages was around twice the weight designated by the original design, because extra reinforcing concrete had been added to the span to support increased traffic from changed approach roads.

He absolved Edward Olencewicz of any blame. 'There is no evidence to suggest that the driver or any member of the crew were at fault in any way. In fact, they appear to have carried out their duties in a careful and conscientious manner.' Nor was the locomotive unsafe, if it had been properly serviced, and he had been assured that it had been.

Finally he lauded the efforts of the rescuers, saying the rescue operation was organised and carried out without delay and 'in a most efficient manner under extraordinarily difficult and dangerous conditions ... Little could be suggested by way of improvement.'

Some good came out of the disaster. Judge Staunton's lambasting prompted the New South Wales government to immediately earmark $200 million to upgrade the shambolic railway system to a safe operational standard. Later in 1977, largely as a result of the traumas of those associated with Granville, the National Association of Loss and Grief (NALAG) was formed to promote community and professional education in loss, grief, bereavement and trauma. And 262 of those who worked bravely and tirelessly amid the death and destruction of that terrible day at Granville were awarded State medals 'in recognition of outstanding service'. Five heroes were awarded the Queen's Gallantry Medal, including Dr Ernest Pedersen and Sergeant Joe Beecroft, and five, including Constable John Wilson, received the Queen's Commendation for Brave Conduct.

In the months after the crash, the Granville Memorial Trust was established to honour the victims and lobby for improved rail safety. The prime mover was John Hennessy, a painter and grower of roses, who pressed Premier Wran for three years to create a 'living memorial' for the victims. Today Hennessy is president of the Trust. Every year on 18 January, he and the families and friends of those who died, as well as others whose lives were changed by the tragedy, gather at Granville Memorial Park and march through the streets of Granville to the Bold Street bridge. Prayers are said, and memories shared, and eighty-three roses – one for each person who died – are dropped from the bridge onto the tracks below.

CHAPTER 14

THE ALICE SPRINGS BALLOON PLUNGE

13 AUGUST 1989

On that bright, still dawn, five hot-air balloons lifted off together from Santa Teresa Mission Road, 13 kilometres south of Alice Springs, and floated high into the blue Central Australian sky. Just before lift-off the pilot of one of the balloons, Michael Sanby, for a joke, took out his trumpet and entertained his passengers with a rendition of 'The Last Post'.

In colourful formation, the balloons wafted across the desert. The morning was later described as 'beautiful flying weather'. An excited group of twelve to fifteen adventurers, each of whom had paid around $95 for the ride, was on each balloon. An hour into the joy flight, 600 metres above the ground, 25 kilometres south-east of Alice, one balloon clipped the basket of the balloon flying close above it, the balloon piloted by the trumpet-playing Sanby. The lower balloon, its envelope deflated and flapping crazily, plunged to earth on Undoolya Station. The pilot and all twelve passengers were killed.

The wicker basket on the six-storey high balloon, serial no. VHNMS, owned and operated by Toddy's Ballooning of Alice Springs, disintegrated on impact. One occupant was tossed clear on impact and died; the others had been smashed so forcibly into the shattered basket that it took ambulance officers and rescue workers three hours to free the bodies. Littered in the red dirt and mulga around the crash site were liquid propane gas cylinders, struts, an altimeter, clothing, shoes and provisions and the collapsed envelope whose striking black and red colours made the tragedy seem even sadder.

A man who was onboard the balloon which was bumped by VHNMS said he did not see the approaching collision. There was a dreadful jolt from below and all looked down to see the top of the other balloon tearing apart and feel a great rush of air. People on his balloon screamed, but he could hear no sound from the stricken balloon, which descended rapidly despite the pilot frantically trying to ignite another burner to reinflate the envelope and arrest its fall.

A shaken Ken Watts, manager of Aussie Ballooning, who was flying another balloon in the vicinity and saw it all, told reporters:

> I saw the balloon deflate quickly and become semi-deformed. I couldn't believe what I was seeing when the balloon ... plummeted straight down to earth. ... It was a sickening sight. I just followed it visually down ... until the load struck the ground. I don't know how long it took to fall. When you see something as horrific as that was, it seemed to take an eternity but it might have been a very short space of time.

Added another, 'They must have known what was going to happen ... they would have been terrible seconds.'

One eyewitness said that when the balloon hit the ground and sent up clouds of red dust, it reminded him of an atomic bomb exploding.

The media, clamouring to report on Australia's worst ballooning accident, converged on the premises of the operator Toddy's Ballooning in Todd Street, Alice Springs. Michael Sanby, the pilot of the balloon which VHNMS had struck and the manager of Toddy's, was in 'deep shock' and unable to be interviewed. There was a blackboard in the window, proclaiming, 'Balloons every morning ... Pick-up and drop-off at your hotel ... A la carte breakfast ... great fun for everyone.' The passengers had been picked up at their hotels that morning at 5 a.m.

Poignant details of some of those who died on 13 August were released. Daphne Overton of Dubbo had been on a bus trip in Central Australia and the balloon trip was a prized part of the package. Garry and Jennifer Dover of Wentworth Falls in the Blue Mountains of New South Wales signed on while on holidays, even though Gary had told his mother that he was not keen to go aloft. Peter Reid, of Telegraph Point on the mid-north coast of New South Wales, lost his wife Belinda and mother-in-law Claire Taylor. Priben Jacobsonen, 26, of Denmark was on the trip of a lifetime.

Hot-air balloons function when liquid propane gas is ignited in a burner and the flame is injected within the envelope, heating the air inside it. The hotter the air inside the envelope, the faster and higher the balloon rises. To lower the balloon, the pilot releases hot air from a vent at the top of the envelope. The pilot steers by catching prevailing winds.

The catastrophe stunned Australia. Before the Alice Springs crash there had been just one balloon fatality, despite people going aloft in burgeoning numbers. The Australian ballooning industry was licensed and regulated by the Civil Aviation Authority and had more stringent safety measures than any other ballooning industry in the world. Balloons were regularly inspected for airworthiness and pilots had ongoing oral and written examinations and physical check-ups. Although the pilot of the doomed balloon, 24-year-old Melburnian Antony Fraser, had only been with Toddy's for two months, he was considered an excellent pilot, described by a colleague as 'a young, adventurous, athletic bloke who had done everything: abseiling, hang-gliding ... everything.' Toddy's suspended all flights pending an investigation by the Civil Aviation Authority and the Bureau of Air Safety.

Meanwhile, after so long without a crash, in the months after the Alice Springs balloon disaster there was a spate of ballooning accidents. In October, six occupants of a joy flight balloon were injured when fierce winds dashed their balloon into a mountainside north-west of Melbourne. Days later, the pilot of a balloon and one of his three passengers were killed when the balloon became entangled with high-voltage power lines near Mudgee, New South Wales. The pilot, Ross Spicer, was electrocuted while trying to lift the unconscious Christine McDonald from the wicker basket. McDonald died of her injuries on the way to hospital. Then, almost incredibly, just three days later, on 14 October, balloon pilot David Bowers was electrocuted when his balloon came into contact with power lines at Cessnock, New South Wales. A passenger, Gabriel Leslie, died too after she jumped from the basket 25 metres above the ground. Not surprisingly, across the land, people were suddenly loath to go aloft.

On 28 November, after the investigation, the Bureau of Air Safety announced that in its view the pilots of both balloons were at fault. The pilot of the higher balloon, Michael Sanby, did not give way to the lower balloon as the operations manual stipulates. Nor did his balloon carry the mandatory instrument package. And Antony Fraser, pilot of the balloon that fell, had not checked the position of the higher balloon before he rose.

Although both balloons were equipped with ultra-high-frequency radios, neither had contacted the other.

Michael Sanby was arrested in Perth in August 1990, as he was attempting to depart Australia for Zimbabwe. He was charged with the manslaughter of the thirteen who lost their lives. Alice Springs coroner Denis Barritt said Sanby, a 36-year-old South African, had been 'grossly negligent' by failing to keep a proper lookout while his balloon was descending. He did not give warning that he was going to descend, had no instruments fitted, and he was flying an un-airworthy balloon.

Coroner Barritt was highly critical of some elements of the ballooning industry, and noted that the Civil Aviation Authority had given commercial licences to unworthy applicants. As well as declaring that the Authority should be more selective in granting licences, he recommended that commercial ballooning be restricted to controlled air space (at the time, only around half of the operators did so). He said that the Authority should take more of an interest in commercial ballooning and ensure that economic forces did not lead to operators cutting safety corners. Also, commercial balloons should not take off when the ground wind speed exceeded 5 knots, or if weather conditions seemed likely to create flying problems.

In Darwin Supreme Court during Sanby's 13-week trial, Justice Sir William Kearney found that the disaster had occurred

> as a result of a collision between its envelope and the basket of a hot air balloon piloted by the accused. The basket of [Sanby's] balloon penetrated the envelope of Mr Fraser's balloon and somehow tangled with a rope mechanism inside that envelope; this led to a Velcro-attached panel in the envelope coming off, with the result that there was then a big gap at the top of Mr Fraser's envelope through which the hot air in that envelope rapidly escaped, leading to the collapse of the envelope and to the balloon plummeting some 2000 feet to the ground.

On 2 December 1992, Sanby was found not guilty of manslaughter, but guilty of the lesser charge of committing a dangerous act, in that he had exhibited a 'cocksure' attitude to balloon flying, and that he 'failed to keep a proper lookout for a period of 30 seconds [when the other balloon had been hidden from view] and that the failure seriously endangered the lives of those below'. Justice Kearney sentenced Sanby to two years in prison, with a non-parole period of eight months.

Sanby appealed the verdict on the grounds that the lower balloon had risen rapidly, and in 1993, the Appeal Court in Darwin quashed his conviction, declaring the tragedy 'an unavoidable accident'.

CHAPTER 15

THE NEWCASTLE EARTHQUAKE

28 DECEMBER 1989

There is never a good time for an earthquake, but when a quake devastated Newcastle between Christmas and New Year in 1989, just as the New South Wales industrial city was putting its feet up after a hard year's toil, it seemed particularly cruel. Large sections of the city centre of Newcastle and surrounding towns of Hamilton and Cooks Hill were laid waste. Thirteen died, and more than 160 were injured. Nine people died when the Newcastle Workers Club crashed down, and three citizens of Hamilton were killed when sections of walls or buildings fell on them.

Australia's worst earthquake – which lasted, according to reports, up to forty-eight seconds including the aftershocks, and registered 5.6 on the Richter scale – impacted at 10.27 a.m. The ground trembled violently, buildings swayed and cracked and sections of them toppled, raining glass and bricks onto pedestrians and vehicles. People, many screaming and panic-stricken, ran from the falling debris. Others sheltered under cars and tables, embraced their loved ones and strangers and prayed. Afterwards, people wandered befuddled, bleeding and dusty. Said one, 'I thought a bomb had exploded and then I realised that this was even worse.' And another: 'This sort of thing simply doesn't happen in Australia.'

The CBD, and especially the main thoroughfare, Hunter Street, had been packed with people on holidays and those cashing in on the post-Christmas sales when the ground buckled and bucked beneath their feet.

The people died at Newcastle Workers Club when they were buried beneath a collapsed 300-tonne brick retaining wall and a concrete mezzanine floor slab. Rescuers with heat-seeking devices searched for bodies there and in the ruins of other buildings. More than 60 000 buildings sustained what would amount to more than $4 billion of damage. It was estimated that 75 per cent of multi-storey buildings and 50 per cent of single-storey buildings had been badly damaged. Essential services such as electricity, water, gas and telephones were cut.

In hindsight, the earthquake was a disaster waiting to happen. The city had been struck by powerful earthquakes before, in 1868 and 1925, so it was a known quake zone. Many of the buildings were constructed of flimsy timber and unreinforced masonry and dated back to the 1860s, and had been inadequately maintained. Mortar holding brickwork together had been eroded over the years by the sea air and industrial pollution. The 1979 earthquake building code did not stipulate that earthquake-resistant design regulations for new buildings be enforced in Newcastle, nor was it decreed that old buildings be strengthened to stand the shocks of a quake. Yet the code did advise – although not order – owners 'to do more than just provide the minimum strength'.

Certainly, a number of buildings in and around Newcastle were in no condition to withstand the quake of 1989. And, as a feature article in the Australian Bureau of Statistics *2008 Yearbook* pointed out, the foundation soils in Newcastle were a problem.

> In the inner parts of the city these were alluvium, some of it dredged from the Hunter River, other parts were underlain by former courses of the river now filled either naturally over time or for housing developments. Ground shaking on sedimentary layers may be amplified relative to that on bedrock at frequencies which correspond to the natural frequencies of buildings so damage is exacerbated.

In 2007, US researcher Christian Klose, from Columbia University's Lamont-Doherty Earth Observatory, published a paper whose premise was that underground coal mining over centuries had further destabilised the earth around Newcastle and made it more vulnerable to earthquake. Geo-mechanical pollution – the removal of millions of tonnes of coal and four times as much water – had, he said, significantly changed the stress field in the earth's upper crust below the Newcastle coalfield since 1801.

The day of the quake – 28 December – was pension payment day, and the Workers Club was abuzz with bingo games and the clatter of poker machines. Many patrons were excited by the prospect of that evening's Crowded House and Split Enz concert. The club, one of the social hubs of the city, was decorated to the nines with streamers and tinsel.

People described how the building wobbled and shook, then seemed to fall to pieces all around them. The roof literally caved in. Those who died stood no chance. Most of the dead and injured were in the first floor poker machine room. 'The whole place just shook,' recalled Jenny Matthews, who was hospitalised with a broken thigh bone, broken ankle and injuries to her arm. 'All the lights went out and then the floor crashed. I ended up in the car park two floors below … and I could hear other people around me screaming and crying. I was shouting out for help. I just thought I was going to die.' Jessie Pinfold, 79, was on her way to collect her winnings when, she told reporters, 'the lights went out and I can remember falling down. It was pitch black and we were all singing out for help.'

Within twenty minutes of the quake, scores of police, firefighters and army personnel were at the scene. Teams of doctors and rescue personnel were on hand. Some twenty local ambulances were despatched. Up to fifty ambulances from all over New South Wales, as well as helicopters and air ambulances, were soon on the way from Sydney. Prime Minister Bob Hawke commandeered a New South Wales government helicopter to whisk him to Newcastle from Kirribilli House in Sydney, where he was relaxing. Premier Nick Greiner cut short his Hawaiian holiday to rush home. Hospitals in Newcastle and Sydney were placed on emergency standby, but the ability of Royal Newcastle Hospital, the Mater Hospital and the John Hunter Hospital to cope with the influx of earthquake victims was limited by the severe structural damage each had sustained, and in fact wings would need to be demolished in the weeks to come.

For the next days, rescue workers, including cavers, picked their way through the debris, hoping for signs of life. There were no miracles. Among the fatalities was Carol Coxhell, 49 – described as 'a beautiful person … the sort of person who'd do anything to help someone' – who had worked at the club for twelve years. She was supervising in the poker machine room when the earthquake hit. Husband and father John O'Shanassy, 30, had brought equipment for that night's concert and was waiting in the auditorium for road crew to help him unload his truck when the roof fell on him. At his funeral on 4 January, a convoy of fourteen prime movers driven by truck driver friends accompanied his hearse. Eileen Werren, 69, was at the club renewing her membership when crushed by the concrete slab. Her son said she only visited the establishment once each year, to pay her dues. She would have left earlier and been spared had a bus strike not delayed her plans. Happy-go-lucky Barry Spark, 60, was the club's maintenance man. His body was located in the basement. His son Glenn also worked at the club. Said Glenn's brother Dean to a reporter from the *Sydney Morning Herald*:

> ... it was almost a double tragedy for my family. If Glenn hadn't called in sick that day he most probably would have been in the room with the poker machines ... Dad's death has hit Glenn really hard because he worked with him and he knows the rescue workers could have found his body too.

Much luckier was Mary Ironman, 68, who was dragged alive from under tonnes of debris two days after the disaster. Her leg had been impaled when her poker machine fell on it, and she was struck by rubble from a nearby wall. 'I've given birth to children,' she said, 'but that was nothing to the pain I was in. It was unbearable ... Everyone was screaming in pain and calling for help but I realised that if I didn't stop shouting I wouldn't have any breath to breathe. There was dust everywhere and it was so dark.'

Among the many heroes was Norm Duffy, a 62-year-old retired boilermaker. He and his wife Miriam were playing the 5-cent poker machines when the Workers Club collapsed. He suffered terrible injuries to his legs and arms and was knocked unconscious. 'I had two poker machines on top of my legs, pinning me down, and a lady lying across my chest,' he recalled to a reporter from his hospital bed. 'There was another woman lying next to me, but I couldn't see my wife. I knew there was a woman underneath me. That must have been her. She was moaning for a short time, and then nothing. I kept calling out for her but she didn't answer.' Miriam had been crushed to death.

Duffy, despite being in tremendous pain, 'was a real hero', said paramedic Alan Playford. In the darkness, he stroked the women's foreheads, held their hands and continually reassured them that they were going to live. 'He was the only source of light down that hole.' Duffy also kept repeating, 'I can see the sun. We'll all be out in the sunshine soon.'

Eventually he lapsed into unconsciousness, and for a moment he was clinically dead. A rescue team removed the woman on top of him. Then it was his turn to be cut free. The paramedics revived him. Twenty years later, Playford was still in awe of the courage of Norm Duffy, who died in 2008:

> Here's this man covered in centimetres thick of cement dust talking to those around him and encouraging them despite the horrific conditions he was trapped in. So his stoic approach to his predicament really transformed us, those who were watching on and watching what he did. He's just an amazing man.

Rescue workers deployed to find and extricate bodies at the club swear they will never get over the sights they saw. Two days after the quake, six bodies remained beneath the fallen concrete slab. Workers manning giant tractorvators and with jackhammers toiled night and day breaking up sections of the slab – the noise of the metal biting into concrete was deafening – and trucks carted the rubble away. Salvation Army members, unable to do more to help for now, sat together and prayed. The stench of rotting bodies filled the summer air. Reported Candace Sutton of the *Sydney Morning Herald*:

> The bodies lay in an amazing hotchpotch of rubble: Christmas tinsel, twisted steel girders, stacks of vinyl padded chairs, windows, walls, air-conditioning ducts, battered poker machines, around \$20 000 in coins, and, perched on the side of a crumbled bathroom, a shiny red ladies' handbag.

It was 31 December before the last body was recovered.

More than 1500 Novocastrians were left homeless when their houses and apartments were destroyed or rendered uninhabitable. An emergency relief centre with counselling, food, shelter and water was established at the gymnasium of Broadmeadow High School, with 4000 availing themselves of the services. The Salvation Army and St Vincent de Paul coordinated food and clothing donations. Also rolling up their sleeves and weighing in were the police, fire brigade, ambulance officers, doctors and nurses, the Volunteer Rescue Association, Newcastle City Council employees, the Army, health workers, city officials and council workers, electricity, water and gas supply and telephone workers, and volunteers from the public. Companies such as TNT gave money and trucks to transport people and belongings from destroyed homes. The federal government and the state governments all pledged relief and rebuilding funds. A donation arrived from sister city Newcastle in England.

SES rescue and administration teams covered themselves with glory, working in horrific conditions for up to thirty-four hours without a break. 'I couldn't begin to name all the SES men and women who volunteered their time over the past five days,' said Lower Hunter State Emergency Services Divisional Officer Bob McGregor-Skinner on 2 January.

> They have worked such long hours, have lived in makeshift accommodation and have worked without a great deal of rest. Some of them had no toilet facilities, they had to make huge sacrifices to help the earthquake victims. The teamwork and comradeship which exists is unbelievable. People don't realise that they do all this in their own time and at a time of year when some of them would be away on holidays.

Entertainer Su Cruickshank, whose long career had begun at Newcastle Workers Club, turned the New Year's Day Midsummer Jazz Concert she was hosting in Sydney's Domain into a benefit concert for those affected by the earthquake. A short film of the city in ruins was screened before the concert began and Salvation Army officers moved through the crowd with buckets to collect donations. The crowd gave freely. The fundraising Premier's Concert at the Sydney Entertainment Centre in February, starring Peter Allen and Olivia Newton-John and with Prince Edward as guest of honour, raised tens of thousands of dollars for relief. Money flooded into the Newcastle Lord Mayor's Relief Fund – it would realise more than $8 million, but legal recriminations would ensue over its distribution – and ANZ banks Australia-wide accepted donations from the public. The Salvation Army and St Vincent de Paul outlets became collection points for clothing and blankets for the survivors. People rushed to give blood.

On the twentieth anniversary of the earthquake, the Newcastle *Herald* published a commemorative supplement, *Newcastle Earthquake: A Time of Heroes*. The heroes lauded included

> Stephen Pirie, an unemployed New Lambton man who turned up at the devastated Newcastle Workers Club with soft drinks for the thirsty rescue workers; SES welfare officer Gwen Myles and her volunteers who provided rescue workers with more than 1600 meals a day; bus driver Eddie King, who stopped in Beaumont Street and volunteered to transport injured people to hospital, singing at the top of his voice as he did so to cheer his passengers; and pensioner John Milne, who rescued his wife from the Workers Club then crawled back into the darkness seeking other victims.

Less admirable were the actions of men caught by police looting the Mayfield Bi-Lo supermarket, and of the 34-year-old man who was arrested stealing forty-one cases of beer from the Workers Club even as the bodies of the club members remained in the debris. Police and army personnel consequently set up road blocks and allowed only those providing essential services into the city. In the weeks to come, police compiled a lengthy shame file. It included the fake insurance assessors who stole goods from homes they had entered ostensibly to check damage, tradesmen charging exorbitant prices for essential work, bogus structural engineers charging a $75 fee to inspect homes for damage, landlords increasing rental prices for those made homeless by the quake, and removalists charging double their normal fee to move furniture from homes. There were also accusations that many heritage-listed homes and buildings, such as the George Hotel and Carrington Chambers, were demolished unnecessarily so greedy developers could construct high-rise buildings in their place.

Fears of a pest plague were realised when hordes of cockroaches were disturbed by the earthquake and the demolition work and invaded homes.

Flies, mice and rats converged on the piles of garbage and food that had spoiled during the power cuts.

Rodents and insects were not the only pests to invade Newcastle. Ignoring the warning of Newcastle Council and police to stay away, sightseers with cameras and maps wandered among the ruins, hampering the work of those with emergency passes who were trying to clean up and restore order. A mob gathered where once had stood the Newcastle Workers Club. 'Newcastle people are still too traumatised to look at the sites,' student Louise Greenland told a reporter. 'That's the last thing this place needs. The rubberneckers and tourists are coming in and looking at our misfortune while all we are trying to do is get on with our lives.'

Hardly a home or office block escaped structural damage, and in January the work of demolishing buildings that were too smashed to be braced and rebuilt began. Houses, schools, hotels, churches, apartment blocks, hospital wings, fell to the wrecking ball. One man refused to leave his home. He sat amid the rubble weeping and told demolishers that he had lived in the house for fifty years and had no intention of living anywhere else. After some hours, he allowed himself to be led away.

Kim Britton, whose home was battered by the earthquake, expressed her devastation in the Newcastle *Herald* on 1 January.

> The broken crockery and fallen plaster are all cleaned up, the shattered masonry swept aside and the bricks from a fallen chimney tidily stacked behind the house. Novocastrians everywhere have worked hard to clear away the debris of Thursday's earthquake but there still lingers the aftershock of fear and dislocation. Even those lucky enough to have sustained no damage to their homes still share the common feeling of devastation. It's a feeling of frailty, vulnerability, the disorientation of accident victims multiplied by several hundred thousand. The enormity of our helplessness in the face of the quake has left a legacy of heightened mortality ... The phone keeps ringing and the usual 'How are you' takes on a new significance. Yesterday morning I opened a cabinet to discover that my grandmother's fine old sherry glasses had cracked.

> Each day so far has brought fresh discoveries of cracked walls, of cupboards previously unopened bearing a jumble of disrupted possessions ... There is a physical ache that accompanies our own human aftershock. The knotted shoulders and deep-down ache in the bones that might accompany a bad dose of flu are part of post-earthquake-itis. As is the missed heartbeat when a too-loud truck rumbles by or the washing machine shudders in the spin cycle. There is a sense of unreality, an exhausted sadness ... With the heart of the city in ruins, there is no centre to the community.

State Coroner Waller summed up the disaster and Newcastle's reaction to it, when he declared, 'Feats of gallantry were numerous and it is uplifting for the rest of Australia to see how a community like Newcastle can respond to a shocking calamity.'

On the evening of 19 January, 1000 people packed into Newcastle's Christ Church Cathedral to remember the victims of Australia's worst earthquake. There were loved ones, rescuers, police and medicos, and ordinary citizens. Prime Minister Hawke and Governor-General Bill Hayden came with their wives, and Premier Greiner attended. The names of the thirteen who perished were read aloud and a candle lit to commemorate each person. Symbolic objects were placed at the altar: building equipment, a length of rope, a tree, bread and water. 'Newcastle people are tough and resilient,' said the Archbishop of Newcastle, the Right Reverend Alfred Holland, in his address. 'They are not strangers to hardship. As a result of this earthquake we will have the chance not only to recover, but to renew both ourselves and our community.' He quoted the words of poet James McAuley:

> Winter will grow dark and cold
> Before the wattle turns to gold.

CHAPTER 16

THE BOONDALL BUS CRASH

24 OCTOBER 1994

'It was a nightmare and everything happened so fast,' said one survivor of Queensland's worst bus crash. 'There were people screaming and the bus seemed to roll. Before I knew it, it was on its side.'

That morning back in 1994, the Wide Bay Tours coach was carrying a high-spirited group of fifty-two passengers, most of them elderly women, good friends and members of a widows' support group – the Association of Civilian Widows – which organised outings for women whose husbands had passed away. They were on a shopping trip from their home town, Maryborough in south-eastern Queensland, to Logan Hyperdome on the southern edge of Brisbane. On the way there had been sing-alongs and banter and excited chat about the bargains that would be had at the Hyperdome.

Then, at 10.10 a.m., the coach veered off the southbound lane of the Gateway Arterial Road, 150 metres south of the Sandgate Road overpass at Boondall, an outer north Brisbane suburb. It hurtled across the median strip, overturned and then slid on its side across the northbound lanes and plummeted, tumbling over and over, down a steep embankment. Eleven women and one child of 2, a boy who had been travelling with his pregnant mother and grandmother, were killed and the remaining thirty-nine passengers and the driver suffered either major or minor injuries in the crash. Many of those who died were crushed in their seats; others were killed when they were flung from windows onto the road. Reported Queensland Police Service spokesman Brian Swift from the scene of the crash:

> The coach somehow left the southern two-lane highway just after coming over a slight rise. It crossed a 2 ft deep ditch between the north- and south-bound carriageways, came out of the ditch and slewed across the northbound lanes, demolishing a telephone booth and falling. It then ploughed savagely down a 15 ft embankment into a dry swamp.

Beth Ross, in her seventies, was one of the survivors and later, from her Redcliffe hospital bed, where she was being treated for cracked ribs and a grazed arm, she was incredulous that she had been spared, suffering only relatively minor injuries, when so many of her friends had died. 'I was the luckiest of the whole busload. I've known all those ladies for years. Everyone was a good sport.'

When the coach driver lost control of the vehicle, she said,

> I didn't realise what was happening until I was picking myself up from the floor. The bus wobbled and tipped itself over on its side. I felt two bumps but I can't remember any noise. I had fallen over another lady and she had fallen over the seat and fallen on her neck, which was very sore. It's a wonder everybody wasn't killed. It's something I'll never forget.

Motorists who pulled over and ran to the smoking, bloody wreckage to help free the trapped and injured were met with terrible scenes. 'There seemed to be bodies everywhere,' said Barry Comer. 'One woman we helped get out had her right arm torn off just below the elbow. She was screaming, "Please help me! Please help me!" Another man had his head jammed in an air vent in the roof of the bus.' Another Samaritan, Bill Blackwood, called the roadside carnage 'the worst thing I have ever seen. There were people screaming and we were pulling people out from under dead bodies'. 'There were bodies lying everywhere,' said another. One remarked, 'The inside of that bus was a bloody mess. I never want to see anything like that again'.

Within minutes of the crash, the emergency centre at Royal Brisbane Hospital swung into action and the centre's disaster plan ran smoothly. Teams of doctors and nurses were despatched to the site by road and helicopter.

The forty surviving occupants were dragged and cut from the twisted metal and taken in ambulances to Prince Charles Hospital, Redcliffe Hospital, the Mater Hospital, Princess Alexandria Hospital and Royal Brisbane suffering shock, fractures, cuts and abrasions. They were traumatised and disoriented, and some had no idea where they were or what had happened. Others hysterically asked about the condition of fellow passengers. When the living had been cared for, the fifty police and other rescuers – including firefighters, ambulance officers, SES volunteers and members of the public – turned their attention to the dead. A makeshift morgue was established on the roadside and the grisly task began of freeing the bodies and laying them in the morgue. Then rescuers were faced with the terrible task of trying to match severed limbs with bodies.

The motorists who had stopped found themselves vital links in the rescue team. Ambulance officers handed each a trauma pack comprising bandages, gloves and first aid items and directed them to do what they could. Some were amazed by the number of motorists who did not stop to help but kept driving.

The coach driver, Richard Provyn, who was dragged moaning and shaking from the crumpled vehicle, in shock and with a fractured hip, beseeched rescuers to tell him of the fate of his passengers. He told police that just before the bus veered, he had felt a 'shuddering' and that his steering had failed. It had been his first accident in twenty years of driving coaches.

All lanes of the Gateway Arterial Road were closed until 9.30 that evening, and the coach transported to a police garage for examination.

From the moment news of the crash reached Maryborough, the town was in deepest mourning at the loss of many of its best-known and most popular citizens. 'These women have given so much over the years, caring for each other and raising money for charity,' despaired the mayor of Maryborough, Alan Brown. 'A day which should have been enjoyed has turned into a tragedy.'

A non-denominational memorial service was conducted at St Mary's Catholic Church. 'We offer our prayers to God, because we do not understand,' said the Reverend John Evans. The men, women and children of Maryborough, as well as Queensland Premier Wayne Goss, were in tears as the community came together to offer prayers and hymns for the victims.

Goss broadcast his condolences to the loved ones of the victims and the people of Maryborough.

> On behalf of all Queenslanders, let me extend sympathy to those who lost family members or loved ones in this tragedy. That so many people were killed or injured has shocked and saddened the state. Let me offer condolences to the entire community of Maryborough, which has suffered a heavy loss.

Two members of that community, Fred and Olive Stevens, both 90, were interviewed by Brisbane's *Courier-Mail* reporter Neil Breen. Their great friend and Treasure Street neighbour Eileen Walter had been one of the fatalities. Though 74 herself, Eileen had looked out for the Stevenses. Olive Stevens said:

> Yesterday her cat came over here in the morning and stayed all day. We knew something was wrong. We've been crying ever since we heard that she had passed away. Every morning and every afternoon she would spend time with us and cared for us. I don't know what we are going to do. My eyesight is gone, my hearing is gone, my body is going – I should have died 10 years ago. Now it's Olive who's gone. I don't know what to do.

The Stevenses had paid the $26 for their friend's bus ticket, to thank her for all she had done for them. 'She never wanted to take our money but we were pleased to pay for her ticket each month when the Civilian Widows' Association went on their shopping trip.'

The day after the crash there was uproar in the media over the fact that the bus had not been equipped with seat belts, which would undoubtedly have saved the lives of at least a number of the passengers who were thrown out and onto the road. A spokesperson for the bus' manufacturer, Motor Coach Australia, who built the bus for Wide Bay Tours, defended the safety record of his company's 'custom built and hand built' buses. The vehicles were rigorously inspected, as per government regulations, every six months. Motor Coach Australia would comply with the government regulations calling for all coaches built after 1 July 1995 to be fitted with seat belts, but said it was impractical to suggest that existing buses without belts be modified immediately. 'People are always blowing their heads off in the media about putting seat belts in all buses but it's not just a matter of putting them in. They have to be attached to the frame of the bus.' And to accommodate seat belts, he continued, the old seats had to be replaced by stronger seats.

A crash survivor, speaking out on condition that she not be identified, told a reporter from the *Courier-Mail* that in her opinion the bus that crashed was in poor condition. 'I don't think that bus should have been on the road. The air-conditioning wasn't working. The microphone wasn't working too well. When pensioners have a trip, [bus proprietors] give them a cheaper rate, but they don't put their good buses on.' These allegations were strongly denied by Motor Coach Australia.

When the wreckage of the coach was inspected, it was found that a mechanism connected to one of the axles had broken free. 'If that locating rod let go, the axle would swing back on the right-hand side, effectively steering the axle to the right,' said investigator and accident expert Geoff McDonald. That, it was decided, was the probable cause of the accident, and backed up driver Provyn's contention that there was a shudder and then the steering malfunctioned. There were also cracks in the coach's suspension gear.

Checks were made on seventy-eight coaches that were of similar design to the death coach, and eight were found to have serious defects.

Meanwhile, Maryborough struggled to come to terms with its loss. As one resident pointed out, 'We have lost more than ... citizens. We have lost ... charity workers, good neighbours, old and dear friends whose value to our community was priceless.'

CHAPTER 17

LANDSLIDE AT THREDBO

30 JULY 1997

The popular ski resort of Thredbo, 1365 metres above sea level in New South Wales' Kosciuszko National Park, was in the midst of its fortieth birthday revels when the mountainside collapsed and slid. Those who heard it described the noise as being like that of an explosion, a freight train, a tornado, an F-111 taking off, or a tidal wave. One eyewitness said that to her it looked like a giant had taken a huge bite out of the mountain.

At around 11.30 p.m. on Wednesday, 30 July, a steep embankment on the Alpine Way highway at Thredbo subsided, sending tonnes of earth crashing more than 100 metres into the Carinya Ski Lodge, a four-storey hotel. In turn, the lodge was torn from its foundations and careered a further 100 metres down the hill, where it slammed into Bimbadeen Lodge, another tourist hotel, and its adjoining staff quarters. The mountainside and the two destroyed hotels became one horrific landslide, comprising 3500 tonnes of rock, trees, dirt, mangled timber, concrete, furnishings, the vehicles of guests and staff, and human beings, and plummeted on to the bottom of the slope.

Thredbo was declared a regional disaster area, and by 20 past midnight police, doctors and rescue teams, some specialising in mine rescues, had arrived by vehicle or flown in on Navy helicopters. The terrible cries of the trapped could be heard, but faded as the night wore on, leading a policeman to observe, 'It doesn't look good.' And it wasn't. In all, eighteen people – eleven men and seven women – were killed by the initial impact, or died in the rubble.

At dawn on 31 July, when the job of freeing the bodies and rescuing survivors was not yet in full swing, but it was already clear that the death and injury toll would be high, an unwell Prime Minister John Howard addressed the nation from his hospital bed.

> The thoughts and prayers of all Australia are with those people unaccounted for and their families and friends. The horrifying pictures of the scene at Thredbo [which even at that early hour were being broadcast on televisions throughout the land] are a reminder

to all of the fragility of life and reinforce the strength which can be gained from a sense of community in times of national tragedy.

Despite exhaustion and hypothermia in the minus 14 degree Celsius night temperatures – which rose only marginally by day – the rescuers toiled for the next two days, delving through the rubble, hauling survivors free and removing bodies from the ruins and earth. According to the Coroner's report, the first body was taken from the rubble at 8.50 p.m. on 31 July. The injured were taken by ambulance or airlifted to Cooma Hospital which had been stocked with large supplies of the blood that would be needed so badly in the days to come.

For a time, when the rubble was seen and heard to shift, all rescue efforts ceased because the site was deemed too unstable. Glenn Milne, today a renowned journalist and political commentator, was staying with his family at Leatherbarrel Lodge, adjacent to Carinya Lodge. His reporter's instincts came to the fore despite the horror and shock of the disaster. Milne, who himself pitched in to help rescuers, gave a graphic report of the disaster to the *Daily Telegraph*:

> We started the rescue attempts as soon as we evacuated families and children. We got down into the rubble and started clawing away chunks of rubble, concrete. Because of the terraced arrangements, when the lodges came down, cars came down too. There were four or five that I saw come down and there were more just teetering up on the edge of the rubble while we were digging. We heard voices, we heard three separate voices, one definitely a male that we could identify – we couldn't get to them. We could hear two more voices further down. We don't know if they were male or female. We were trying to get to these people. When the rescue services arrived they told us that we had to get out of there and that's what we did. I keep thinking of this word pancake – floors have collapsed one on top of the other as they have come down the hill. An almighty gush of rubble just slid down the hill and collapsed the lodges. It was an almighty roar. There [were] tonnes of concrete, earth, trees. It just

> collapsed down the side of the hill, spilled across the access road to our lodge, the Leatherbarrel, and then further down the hill. There's bedding, personal belongings, everything just sandwiched in there. When it first happened I grabbed my two daughters and wrapped them in doonas and took them down the hill. Since then police have sealed off that area. Police are now saying that the whole area is geographically unstable.

The rescuers, in the fluorescent orange overalls and hard hats that forever will be synonymous with this disaster, threaded their way through the rubble, slowly removing the tonnes of debris virtually brick by brick, rock by rock, so as to avoid starting new landslides, and passing the materials gingerly from person to person in a human chain. The precariously piled rubble was 'like a pack of cards which could collapse with one false move', said one member of a rescue squad.

Later on 31 July, a diamond-tipped concrete cutter arrived, as did thermal imaging cameras to detect a survivor's body heat, seismic detectors and a minuscule fibre optic camera to detect signs of life in the twisted mess. Floodlights were mounted so rescuers could work day and night.

Many of the rescuers were volunteer emergency services personnel, white- and blue-collar workers, students, the unemployed, good Samaritans all, hailing from Sydney, Canberra and the bush. Afterwards, a group of school students wrote to the rescue organisers, summing up the gratitude of the nation: 'To emergency workers and volunteers, we have been watching the Thredbo disaster on television and we would like to express our admiration for the courage, bravery and determination you have shown us.'

On Saturday, 2 August, the list of the known dead was released. Among the sad rollcall were the names of Sally and Stuart Diver. Sally was a 27-year-old resort employee and Stuart, her husband, 27, a ski instructor and part-time firefighter at Thredbo.

Sally Diver, tragically, had passed away, but reports of Stuart's death were, like those of Mark Twain's, greatly exaggerated. Shortly before dawn on 2 August, Steve Hirst was clearing rubble near the middle of the site, with a chainsaw running nearby. In a lull in the noise, he thought he heard something. He asked for the chainsaw to be stopped, lay down on the ground and yelled 'Rescue team working overhead, can you hear me?' There was a murmur from below. 'We called for complete silence on the site,' he said. 'I repeated the call and heard a voice come strongly back to us: "I can hear you".'

Diver was able to give his name. When asked if he'd sustained injuries, he said, 'No, but my feet are bloody cold.'

Stuart Diver, dressed only in shorts and T-shirt, was wedged 2 metres under the ground, lying in his mangled bed in pitch blackness. According to rescue worker Rob Killham, '[Diver] and his wife were in a coffin-like entombment which measured about 2 metres by 160 centimetres by 30 centimetres.'

Diver later told how, between bouts of unconsciousness, he thought of being freed and seeing his loved ones again to sustain his spirit. Nearby lay the body of his wife, whom he had known since they were 16.

An oxygen mask was passed down to Diver, along with a torch and a tube for rehydration fluid. A hot-air pipe was also poked through gaps in the debris until it reached him. The ski instructor – who was suffering internal injuries, damaged limbs, poor circulation, lacerations, bruises and hypothermia – managed to grasp the pipe when it protruded through a small hole, and put it close to his skin. The rescuers painstakingly removed sufficient wreckage, earth and rock to see and make physical contact with Diver.

Paramedic Paul Featherstone – who has proven in various disasters over the years that he has few peers in his field – aided by his colleagues, worked his way through the debris until he was crouched virtually beside Diver, chatting quietly to him, telling him how the rescue was progressing, doing his best to keep his spirits up, and diverting his thoughts from the horror he had experienced. Featherstone later said that Diver was 'in a world of hurt, the worst imaginable'. Said Featherstone to Diver, 'It's going to take a long time, but we'll get out of this. Stick with me and we'll see the mountain again.'

Eleven hours' digging later, Featherstone – who chose to remain beside his man despite the periodic blast of sirens warning that another landslide was imminent as the rubble creaked and shifted ominously – and Diver emerged from the tomb. They were greeted with a roar from the other rescuers that Featherstone says he has only ever heard at a football grand final.

On 4 August, after it was clear that Stuart Diver's rescue would be the one and only miracle, a memorial service was held in Thredbo's John Paul II Ecumenical Centre to honour the eighteen who died in the disaster. Two hundred mourners crammed into the church, including the loved ones of the deceased, rescue workers and Thredbo employees in their various uniforms, Acting Prime Minister Tim Fischer, Opposition Leader Kim Beazley and New South Wales Premier Bob Carr, and hundreds more gathered outside to pray and listen to the service. 'In the days ahead, give us wisdom and understanding because the scars of the mountain we will carry always,' intoned Pastor Clare Singleton. 'May these scars help us remember that true love and life never end.'

On 7 August, the day the final body was recovered and removed from the site, the Thredbo Family Relief Fund was established to help the families of those killed. All governments contributed, as did the ever-generous public.

The Princess of Wales sent a heartfelt letter to the grieving families. Noting that she had been receiving constant updates on the disaster since the mountain collapsed, the Princess, less than a month from her own death, continued:

> Freak storms, floods, earthquakes and landslides, it is difficult to understand why nature can be so awe-inspiring and then so cruel. I cannot begin to imagine the desperation felt by those people first on the scene, frantically trying to dig out any survivors. Then the feeling of hopelessness as their efforts were hampered by the threat of further landslides. The joy, however, when it was realised that there could possibly be one survivor – it seemed as though the whole world held its breath as slowly that one person was pulled from the carnage. I send my deepest sympathy to those who have lost their loved ones, and also to the rescuers and members of the local community, who will be affected by this tragedy for many

> years to come. I am thinking of you all at this very difficult time.
>
> With lots of love from Diana.

At the official inquest, after hearing expert testimony, Coroner Derrick Hand reported that the direct trigger for the landslide was flowing water from a leaking pipe which had destabilised the mountainside, but that ultimate blame lay with the New South Wales National Parks and Wildlife Service and the Roads and Traffic Authority, which had neglected Thredbo for forty years. The Coroner had arrived at the view that the agencies knew of the region's tendency for landslides, but did nothing to shore up the land and avert the disaster.

The Supreme Court of New South Wales largely concurred with Coroner Hand's judgment in December 2004 when, after hearing four months of evidence to decide whether a multi-million-dollar personal injury claim related to the landslide could proceed, it ruled that the cause of the disaster was indeed a leaking mains pipe and a road built on a slope of unstable debris. Giving the green light for Bernd Hecher to sue the New South Wales government, the Roads and Traffic Authority, the National Parks and Wildlife Service and Lend Lease, the company that laid the pipe, Justice Michael Grove ruled that the landslide was 'equally caused by leakage from the main, the marginal instability of the slope above Carinya Lodge, the existence and state of the Alpine Way, and the failure to improve the slope and roadway'.

Justice Grove stressed that there was nothing wrong with the design and construction of the pipe, but 'those responsible for the installation and maintenance of the water main ought to have been aware of the risk of failure and consequent leakage as a result of soil creep. No adequate steps were taken to accommodate and avoid this risk'. Also, the National Parks and Wildlife Service and the Roads and Traffic Authority, who were responsible for the care, control and management of the Alpine Way, 'ought to have been aware of the condition of the slope supporting the road near Carinya [Lodge] but did nothing to stabilise it'.

In 2007, ten years after the landslide, survivor Stuart Diver was interviewed by reporter Luke McIlveen. In the past decade, Diver told

McIlveen, he had remarried and was moving on with his life. He ran a bed and breakfast establishment at Thredbo and gave ski lessons. Still, a large part of his soul and, one suspects, a piece of his heart remained buried in the rubble on the mountainside at Thredbo.

> There's still a massive amount of emotional attachment to everything that happened in Thredbo and I deal with that every day. You don't just draw a line and say, 'Thanks very much, that's the end of that.' Obviously, I lost my wife and 17 other friends ... It is unbelievably difficult. I know other people who have been sole survivors of things. It's hard because you can never, ever sit down with [another] person who survived and talk to them about what went on down there. But I never feel [survivor] guilt. I never asked to be put in that situation, it's just what happened. You can go through life thinking, 'I should feel guilty for this or that', but it's such a wasted emotion.

On 30 July 2007, on the tenth anniversary of Australia's worst alpine tragedy, a commemoration service was held on the now-landscaped slope. Looking at the area where so many died, people who attended mused, you would scarcely know that it had been the site of a disaster. A pianist played '(The Hills Are Alive with) The Sound of Music' and then the names of the lost eighteen were read aloud. Eighteen bells were tolled and eighteen candles lit. Then, as those who had gathered wept, the hymn 'The Lord Is My Shepherd' was sung before the mourners sadly collected their thoughts and filed back down the mountain.

CHAPTER 18

THE SYDNEY HAILSTORM

14 APRIL 1999

On the late afternoon and evening of Wednesday, 14 April 1999, a hailstorm of extraordinary ferocity blitzed the suburbs of Sydney. Tens of thousands of homes, cars, commercial and public buildings and aircraft at Sydney Airport – as well as the people who were caught outdoors – were battered by the cricket ball-sized hailstones that hurtled down from a tumultuous black sky. It felt, said one Sydneysider, 'like the world was ending'.

The 45-minute storm was described by the Commonwealth Bureau of Meteorology as an unusually intense and long-lasting supercell thunderstorm, with hail, rain, lightning, and wind gusting at up to 80 kilometres per hour. It was first detected on meteorologists' radars around 4.30 in the afternoon at the picturesque New South Wales south coast town of Berry, and it then moved north – dumping large quantities of hail as it went – through Kiama, Albion Park and Shellharbour. The storm then turned sharply right and headed out to sea. Those who breathed a sigh of relief breathed too soon. Around 7.30 p.m., as if returning to take care of unfinished business, the storm returned to the coast at Bundeena in the Royal National Park, about 30 kilometres south of the Sydney CBD. There were no more diversions as it powered on across the Sutherland Shire, Botany Bay, then Sydney's eastern suburbs.

When the storm struck the Sydney metropolitan area at around 8 p.m., this writer, at home with his family in Paddington, heard a rumble like that of distant thunder, but constant and sustained. As the storm came closer, the roar became a deafening clatter, sounding for all the world like the hoof beats of an advancing battalion of cavalry. It was the noise of hail crashing down onto the tiled roofs and windows of homes in Rosebery, Kensington, Randwick, Moore Park and southern Paddington. In no time, the hailstones were crashing down on my car, causing fist-sized dents in the duco, and my home, breaking tiles and smashing glass skylights. My family and I forgot about trying to protect furniture and carpets from the hailstones and rain that poured through the ruined roof, and took refuge until the storm passed. The hailstones lay where they fell in our street, too big to melt, and the road and footpath glowed icy-white in the light of the street lamps that still shone. The hailstones were still there well into the following day.

The hailstorm continued relentlessly north, wreaking similar havoc on Rushcutters Bay, Kings Cross, Woolloomooloo, Sydney Harbour (where craft were dented), North Sydney, Manly, the northern beaches and the Palm Beach peninsula. When it reached Broken Bay, shortly after 9 p.m., it finally returned to the sea, this time for good, and by 10 p.m. it had petered out.

Randwick, Botany, Woollahra, Waverley, South Sydney and Marrickville were deemed by the state government to be the worst-hit suburbs. In those areas, more than one million people were directly affected by the storm.

Next morning, people in the areas where the storm had struck awoke to find their suburbs broken and bedraggled. Gardens were destroyed and large branches and piles of leaves from the savaged trees were scattered on the ground. Children emerged into the street carrying hailstones they'd salvaged and kept in the freezer overnight. Most were the size of golf balls, but there were many egg-, orange- and cricket ball-sized hailstones. Some were the size of a grapefruit, or even a rockmelon – an alarming 13 centimetres in diameter. Till then the largest hailstone recorded in New South Wales was 9 centimetres. Some people who were caught outdoors in the storm suffered bruising and abrasions when hit by nature's missiles. A number were treated at hospital casualty wards. Some 15 000 homes were left without power.

The storm arrived without official warning. Every weather report in the evening news bulletins predicted clear weather. Weatherman Tim Bailey of Sydney's Channel 10 told viewers:

> Sunny, sunny, sunny and mainly sunny. It looks like we will have sunshine for the next seven days. The only hiccup … is probably going to be tonight a chance of a shower or two across our rooftops – not much – we will wake up to blue skies tomorrow. In Sydney town and for most of New South Wales we are going to see blue skies and sunshine. It really is a sunny forecast for the next seven days … if the boys at the bureau have got it right.

Clearly, they had not.

The Bureau of Meteorology had known of imminent thunderstorm activity earlier in the afternoon but when the storm passed out to sea just north of Kiama officials assumed it had gone for good. Then, when they realised that the storm had returned and was travelling towards Sydney, they could not broadcast a storm warning because the duty forecaster's phone was tied up with incoming calls from people experiencing the storm on the south coast. The *Daily Telegraph*'s cartoonist Warren Brown depicted a group of weather forecasters at the Bureau of Meteorology, oblivious to the fact that their hail-peppered building lies in ruins around them. One takes a call from a member of the public, turns to his colleagues and says: 'Any of you blokes know anything about a hailstorm?'

Explained the journal *Fire News*:

> Within the storm, temperatures dropped to as low as -50 degrees Celsius at the peak of the 10 000 metre cumulonimbus cloud tops. As the storm moved along the coast, moist sea air was drawn into the storm and strong updrafts blew the air upwards, freezing the moist air, forming hailstones. At the top of the clouds, these hailstones fell out, only to be drawn back in at the bottom, where the process would be repeated over and over as layer upon layer of ice was added to the hail. The intensity of the storm meant that the powerful updrafts could sustain the formation of very large hailstones.

Hailstones can be spheroid, cone-shaped or irregularly shaped, hard or soft, and of varying densities. It was estimated that the hailstones that pounded Sydney and surrounds on 14 April 1999 hit the ground at between 140 and 200 kilometres an hour.

News of damage flooded in to emergency services like despatches from war zones. All across the storm zone, roofs, skylights and windows were smashed by hail and falling trees. Live electrical wires lay in the street. Cars were pocked by the hail as if beaten with hammers. One journalist described the vehicles as looking like 'Bonnie and Clyde's car after it was ambushed by the FBI'. In the only fatality attributed to the storm, a 45-year-old fisherman died when his aluminium dinghy was struck by lightning at Dolans Bay. One 24-year-old man from Lilli Pilli who was crossing the river in a kayak was caught out by the storm. Bombarded with hail, he got out of his craft, overturned it and made it to a buoy, where he took shelter until he was rescued by Lilli Pilli residents. He was later treated for hypothermia. Two men, also from Lilli Pilli, fell through their roofs after they clambered up onto them to try to cover gaping holes.

Some 4000 homes lost power in Narrabeen, Warriewood and Collaroy. Streets flooded when storm drains were clogged with hail. Randwick racecourse was blanketed with hail. Lightning started a fire at a factory in Pagewood. There was hail damage to more than 25 planes at Sydney Airport and flights were cancelled. Garbage bins were swept along flooded streets in Bondi. The Bombora Bar at the Bondi Hotel was awash. Residents of the towering Horizon Hotel in East Sydney cowered as the skyscraper was pummelled by hail, rain and wind. The Alexandria factory of fashion designer Peter Morrissey was devastated. 'The factory was flooded and the power was shorting,' he said. 'It's a nightmare. I haven't cried ... yet.' Morrissey's computers and machinery were destroyed. Opined Kensington home owner and war veteran Don Campbell, whose roof caved in, 'I've been to Borneo and Japan and I've been in rough seas, but I've never seen a storm like this.'

Insurance companies were deluged with calls from policy holders. Most were unable to get through to a consultant, but those who managed to were left in no doubt that they were joining a very long line of customers waiting for a representative to visit and assess the damage and authorise repairs to their ruined property. At least for them there was the promise of restitution, and by the time the damage had been mopped up, insured losses totalled $1.7 billion. People who were uninsured despaired.

In all, according to the *Australian Journal of Emergency Management*, the catastrophe damaged more than 20 000 houses (the damage mainly being holes in roofs) and more than 100 homes were made temporarily uninhabitable. Some 40 000 cars suffered dents and broken windscreens. Many factories and public buildings, including schools, were damaged. And the damage was exacerbated by the wet and windy weather that ensued over the following months. The total cost of the storm, now known as 'the mother of all storms', was estimated at around $2.2 billion.

Thousands of State Emergency Service workers and volunteers (many of them coming from interstate) threw themselves into action helping beleaguered residents, but this was hardly enough to cope. The situation of those whose roofs had been holed was made more difficult in the coming days by heavy rain and high winds. Many tarpaulins were ripped from roofs. Hardware and building supply stores did record business as householders made temporary repairs, at least patching holes in the roof and boarding up windows to ward off the inclement weather.

Sadly, some outlets, knowing their customers were desperate, charged exorbitant prices for tarpaulins, ropes, tiles, aluminium cladding and tools. Some unscrupulous tradesmen raised their prices by up to 200 per cent. One charged a Paddington man $1000 to tie a tarpaulin to his roof. Public outrage at the rampant profiteering by those branded 'vultures of the storm' and 'fiddlers on the roof' prompted urgent intervention from the Minister for Fair Trading, John Watkins. He said:

> Tradespersons are also going door to door and are even setting up card tables in Randwick [racecourse], where queues of distressed people are forming. They are hard to catch, as they set up quickly and don't hang around long. The Department of Fair Trading is investigating and these people who are ripping off those who are in need will be prosecuted to the full extent of the law. Unfortunately there are a small number of unqualified builders, roof repairers and glaziers who take advantage of difficulties and a need for urgent repairs. This is un-Australian.

If people were in doubt about the bona fides of a purported tradesperson, he said, 'take two minutes to check if he has a licence. Those two minutes can save hundreds and hundreds of dollars and hours and hours of heartache.' Community fury forced Energy Australia to back down when the utility announced it would charge a $60 call-out fee to customers whose power had been cut off.

The New South Wales government declared the event an official disaster and, to deal with the enormous mop-up, formed the State Disaster Recovery Committee to unite the relevant government agencies and non-government organisations. Working together were the State Emergency Service, the Premier's Department, the Treasury, the Departments of Community Services, Housing, Public Works and Fair Trading, affected local councils, the Insurance Council of Australia, the Master Builders Association, the Housing Industry Association and small businesses with funds, equipment or expertise to contribute. Deployed in the days after the storm were over 200 000 tarpaulins to the value of $10 million, 280 000 sandbags, 9600 kilometres of rope, safety gear, tools, and over $2 million of equipment hire. According to the *Australian Journal of Emergency Management*, 5006 NSW Rural Fire Service volunteers, 2500 State Emergency Service personnel, 2850 from the NSW Fire Brigade, 750 NSW Parks and Wildlife employees and 650 army personnel were involved in the operation.

Talkback radio stations, keen to perpetuate the anger and so boost ratings, lambasted the efforts of the rescue teams and the state government – unfairly in the eyes of many, because the logistics of repair were enormous and complex. The media criticism was mentioned in the report on the storm published in the *Australian Journal of Emergency Management*, a report that put the herculean efforts of rescuers into fairer perspective.

> By the standards of previous storm responses, the response to Sydney's most damaging storm event ever was an effective one. It started quickly and was sustained for a long period of time under difficult circumstances involving strong media criticism and weather that made operating on roofs unpleasant and sometimes dangerous.
>
> There were, of course, mistakes made, but the SES volunteers and the personnel of the many other agencies involved can be confident that they performed with great credit to themselves and their organisations. The response was a real test of training, of management procedures and of personnel: quite possibly it was the biggest test the SES has ever had in New South Wales.

If, in the aftermath, the SES is made more easily contactable, can manage the media more effectively, is more able to determine the scale of the task at an early stage and can overcome operational shortcomings produced by deficiencies of accommodation and equipment, the result will be an improvement in the organisation's ability to respond effectively when future storms strike.

CHAPTER 19

THE LOCKHART RIVER PLANE CRASH

7 MAY 2005

The twin-engine, 19-seat Aero-Tropics Fairchild Metroliner III sped down the tiny, palm tree-lined airstrip at Bamaga, near the tip of Queensland's Cape York Peninsula, shortly after 11 a.m. on 7 May 2005, bound for the remote Aboriginal community at Lockhart River, where passengers would then connect to a flight to Cairns. The aircraft, which was operated by Brisbane-based airline TransAir, was carrying a precious cargo of fifteen people. The commercial jet, designated Flight 675, was due to touch down at Lockhart River at 11.45. It never made it.

As the aircraft approached Lockhart River from the north-west it flew into a severe storm, with rain, low cloud which had descended to 400 metres, and strong winds. Yet the pilot, Captain Brett Hotchin, sounded unfazed as, at 11.36, he notified air traffic control in Brisbane that he was descending from around 2740 metres into Lockhart River airport. Despite the weather conditions, he reported no problems and said he expected to make a routine landing.

Minutes later, around 10 kilometres from its destination, the plane slammed into the 500-metre-high rainforest-covered ridge known as South Pap and burst into flames.

When rescue workers reached the site, the aircraft – which had crashed about 30 metres below the summit of the mountain – was a charred, still-smoking tangle of metal, luggage and bodies. It was immediately obvious that there was nobody left alive to rescue. 'This is every airline operator's worst nightmare,' said Aero-Tropics proprietor Ric Lippmann.

Next day, investigators – including police, emergency services officers, aircraft structural engineers, body identification experts and officials of the Australian Transport Safety Bureau – gathered on the rugged mountainside in driving rain to pore through what little was left of the Metroliner, to try to discover why it crashed. Foremost in their thoughts was the question of why Captain Hotchin, an experienced pilot who had flown in North Queensland for two decades, was flying his plane so low. Meanwhile, the nation counted the human cost of Queensland's worst air accident in four decades.

Exacerbating the tragedy was the fact that a number of the passengers were high-achieving and beloved members of their community.

Dr David Banks, 55, was one of the nation's finest scientists, the principal scientist with the quarantine authority Biosecurity Australia, and had worked tirelessly to protect Australians from pests and such diseases as Japanese encephalitis, Nipah virus and swine fever. He invented a mosquito trap used widely by cattle farmers in the Northern Territory. 'This is a terrible loss for Australia,' mourned his friend and Biosecurity media officer John Wilson. Banks had been fishing at Bamaga for the past week with his friend Kenneth Hurst, another victim.

Constable Sally Urquhart, 28, a beloved, respected and influential police officer at the Aboriginal community of Bamaga – she had a double degree in law and science, and had pioneered policing in Indigenous communities – also perished. She was flying from Bamaga to attend a constable development training course in Townsville and was due to be married in a fortnight. Her fiancé, Constable Trad Thornton, was also stationed at Bamaga. 'Sally was an outstanding officer and my heart goes out to her family,' said Cairns police Acting Superintendent Michael Keating. She was also lauded as one who performed her duties 'with commitment, professionalism, character, fairness and compassion'. When she died, her family received 870 cards and 300 letters from people whose lives she had touched, and the Queensland Police Service published a book containing the 1500 laudatory emails about her that they had received. In her honour the Service bought a motel in Cairns, called it the Sally Urquhart Residential Facility and used it to accommodate young police officers.

The pilot, Brett Hotchin, 40, was, said his brother Greg, 'one of those likeable guys, everybody loved him. He's probably flown that flight a thousand times – he knew that area like the back of his hand.' An incorrigible larrikin, Hotchin had been wrestling for some years with writing the story of his colourful life – entitled *Flying High Feeling Low, Flying Low Feeling High: Never Let the Truth Get in the Way of a Good Story* – and had hoped to find a publisher. He noted on his web page, '[The book] will, and can only, be published once I have secured my final career position to whatever and wherever that may be. Or death!'

The Injinoo Crocs rugby league team was decimated by the crash. Frank Billy, just 21, was the side's centre three-quarter; Fred Bowie, 25, was the five-eighth; and their fellow victim Gordan Kris, 37, though getting on in years for a footballer, was a vigorous, tough-tackling second rower. 'These boys were the core of the club,' said local official Peter Lui. 'These three blokes, they always brought something special to a game. They were respectable and respected by their community. They loved their footy and they played it fair.' They were travelling to Cairns TAFE, where they were completing courses.

Mardie Bowie, 30, hailed from Bamaga where she was 'the heart and soul' of the community. She had recently been the driving force in establishing a community garden in Bamaga. She was sport and recreation officer for Bamaga Council and Injinoo Aboriginal Council and was the energetic, can-do organiser of the annual Anzac Day parade. She worked with local youth, organising activities for them during school holidays. She had caught the flight as part of her journey to Cairns to attend a course with fellow Bamaga council worker Helen Woosup, a 25-year-old mother of six. Mardie Bowie was Fred Bowie's cousin.

Arden Sonter was the manager of Bamaga Enterprises, which operated the service station and snack bar in Bamaga. It was he who came up with the idea for the community garden in the first place. Sonter was flying to Cairns to meet his wife, Kerry, so that they could drive back to Bamaga together – he didn't want her to undertake the approximately 900-kilometre dirt road journey alone. Ironically, Kerry Sonter had been trying unsuccessfully to contact Arden to tell him not to fly to Cairns, because she had changed her plans.

Rob Brady was an adventurous fellow who had worked as a mechanic in the mining industry in Africa and Papua New Guinea and was currently employed as a guide for Cairns-based Heritage Tours, escorting groups on treks to Cape York Peninsula.

The bodies were extricated from the wreckage in the following days. While they were being examined and identified at the John Tonge Forensic Centre in Brisbane, a memorial service – the first of many for the victims – was held at St Monica's Cathedral in Cairns, and fifteen candles were lit while the congregation prayed. There were many police who came to honour Sally Urquhart, and students from Cairns TAFE to remember their classmates Bowie, Kris and Billy. Police chaplains Reverend Doug Foster and Father George Markotsis addressed the congregation. When Father Markotsis said the crash had ripped the 'sense of security' from the community of Bamaga, sobbing was heard throughout the church. He went on, 'We have lost fifteen people, loved ones, family, friends and colleagues, and the pain of this is real and acute for so many of us. We have lost all their potential, their hopes and their dreams for the future. But we can find comfort in the love we shared with them.'

Mourners collapsed into each other's arms. A number of those who placed floral wreaths at the altar were so distraught that they could not return to their pew unaided. One woman fell to the floor. Assistant Anglican Bishop Jim Leftwich read from *Corinthians* and although he chose words often used to celebrate a wedding, they were apt on this day: 'Without love we are nothing.'

Reverend Foster looked down on the congregation and noted that there was no need to mention the names of those who had died because 'so many of their loved ones have come to share their sorrow.'

Many people from Bamaga chose not to attend the memorial service, but stayed at home to mourn. After what had happened to Flight 675, they were too terrified to board a plane to Cairns.

Father Clive Brook, the priest at Bamaga's St George's Church for more than a decade, said the community would be hurting deeply, but he was confident that their faith would see them through. 'Family values in that town are very strong and they have a strong spiritual awareness. They're beautiful people.' He had known the men who died in the crash and their families.

> The Injinoo people are going to be really shook, shattered. When the news breaks they will wail. That's the only term for it. They will wail as they call out their grief. This is quite a healthy process in contrast to our western approach to death. The extended family ... will then kick into action. They will organise the catering so people are fed and the news is circulated far and wide to the rest of the family, wherever they be, out in the islands, Cairns, Darwin. As

> families come to Bamaga to the funeral they will bring food and money to meet the costs.

As investigations into the crash continued over the following days, some troubling reports emerged. Lately, the doomed aircraft had been experiencing problems, such as when it lost power in one engine while getting ready to take off from Cairns as recently as 20 April. As the month wore on, the blame for the crash was levelled at the pilots, Captain Brett Hotchin and co-pilot Tim Downs. There were reports from within the aviation industry that whoever was at the controls of the Metroliner may have been trying to fly below cloud cover to 'get a visual fix' on the Lockhart River airport runway, and in flying too low had collided with the mountain. The plane was flying at 390 metres when it slammed into the mountain, around 300 metres lower than the stipulated minimum altitude.

An Australian Transport Safety Bureau investigation team sifted through the retrieved wreckage. The black box recording equipment was recovered. Although the voice recorder seemed to have malfunctioned, information had been retained on the plane's altitude, air speed, engine torque and flap positions. The inquiry dragged on, but to the fury of the families of the deceased, the faulty voice recorder prevented the Bureau from arriving at a definitive cause for the disaster.

Also under investigation was the plane's operator, TransAir. Evidence surfaced of seven instances of potentially disastrous safety breakdowns over the years, none of which had been reported. These included the gear failure of a TransAir plane as it was taking off from Bamaga, a cabin pressurisation warning at Cairns, and a burning smell that suffused the cabin near Inverell, in northern NSW. The investigation into TransAir was called off when the airline ceased to operate in December 2006.

Then, on 4 April 2007, the Australian Transport Safety Bureau released its findings. The Bureau had found nineteen factors contributing to the crash. They were that: the co-pilot had limited experience in an instrument landing; the descent speed was too fast; the aircraft was below a safe altitude; the high-speed descent was never corrected; neither pilot saw the mountain before impact; the crew probably had a high workload;

both pilot and co-pilot lost awareness of how low they were; the pilot had a history of operating above speed limits; the Lockhart River runway approach probably created a high workload for pilots; the co-pilot had no formal training for the type of landing being attempted; TransAir's flight crew training had significant limitations; supervision of flights from TransAir's base was poor; TransAir's standard procedures for instrument landings lacked detail; there was no terrain awareness system aboard the plane; TransAir's structure left little room for independent checks and balances; there was a poor safety culture within TransAir; TransAir's chief pilot did not demonstrate a high level of commitment to safety; the Civil Aviation Safety Authority (CASA) provided no guidance to its inspectors; airlines were not required by the regulator to conduct comprehensive risk assessments.

The Bureau's report found that the predominant cause of the disaster was that the pilot in command, either Hotchin or Downs, 'used approach and descent speeds and a rate of descent greater than specified'. Instead of a final approach speed of 240 kilometres per hour, the aircraft was averaging 324 kilometres per hour. Hotchin 'had a history of fast flying … and had been surprised by a high terrain using this same approach 10 days before flying with a different co-pilot'. Also, said the report, 'TransAir's safety management and culture were poor [and] TransAir did not have a structured process for pro-actively managing safety-related risks.' Former TransAir pilot Ken Grant appeared at the hearing and testified that in his opinion Brett Hotchin considered himself 'bullet-proof' and was 'always in a hurry', and that TransAir was 'ready-made for an accident'. He described the airline's former director Les Wright, who held the reins at the time of the crash, as an 'angry ant' who 'virtually wrote all his own rules' and was uncooperative in spending money on safety or training programs.

Apart from apportioning blame, the Bureau's report did not call for punitive action to be taken against those identified.

The Bureau made public its belief that if the plane had been equipped with a terrain alerting warning system the crew would have been given 'the cues or the clues with which to take appropriate action'. The system was due to become mandatory for all aircraft two months after the Metroliner came to grief on South Pap. When this fact was aired at the hearing, relatives in the room wept.

The family of Brett Hotchin was hurt and angered by what they saw as the assassination of his reputation. 'That is the easy way out, to lay the blame on the pilot,' responded Hotchin's brother.

> They are saying it was pilot error but at the end of the day there is no 100 per cent conclusive proof that it was Brett's fault. Brett loved flying, he wanted to work for a big airline, and he was very particular, professional and meticulous about everything he did. This was just such a terrible tragedy.

In March 2007, it was announced that a Coronial Inquest would commence in April. When its findings were released that August, Coroner Michael Barnes found – as had the Australian Transport Safety Bureau – that pilot Hotchin was in the habit of flying too fast and must have realised that his approach into Lockhart River airport was risky. However, Coroner Barnes stressed that he had no interest in making anyone a scapegoat for the crash.

> With all due respect to those families, the making of scapegoats in that manner is not part of my function. I find that CASA could have done more to insist that TransAir improved certain aspects of its operations but I do not believe that the evidence supports a finding that they could reasonably have stopped it from operating or prevented the crash.

The Coroner recommended that CASA hasten the introduction of mandatory crew resource management training, and also called for CASA to improve the efficiency of training and checking organisations for air transport companies. He noted that 'a degree of animosity' existed between CASA and the Australian Transport Safety Bureau, and recommended that the federal Minister for Transport, Mark Vaile, consider engaging an external consultant 'to assess whether high level intervention is warranted'. The Minister pledged to act with alacrity.

Kerry Sonter, wife of crash victim Arden Sonter, branded the 2007 Coronial Inquest report 'a whitewash' and victim Sally Urquhart's father Shane declared that the findings were 'a whole waste of time for all of us'.

The loved ones of the victims wanted to see what they considered to be justice done, and those responsible punished. Shane Urquhart led the push for an inquiry into CASA, and in June 2008 he welcomed the announcement that a Senate Inquiry would be held. Speaking for himself and the families and friends of those who died on Flight 675, he said:

> While the interest of our group has been in the Lockhart River incident where my daughter died, there are many other families out there who have lost loved ones in previous crashes and hopefully they will take the opportunity to participate in the inquiry. I hope CASA's actions over the past five years will be exposed and examined, but I really want an outcome that will assure the public that from now on flying in regional Australia is being supported by a rigorous and best practice safety regime. To date that has not been the case.

In July 2008, the Australian Senate's Rural and Regional Affairs and Transport Committee held their inquiry into the Civil Aviation Safety Authority, and its role in the air disaster. More than sixty submissions from the families and others were considered. In September, the Committee's findings were released. Recommended were: that the Australian government strengthen CASA's governance framework and administrative capability by introducing a board of up to five members to provide enhanced oversight and strategic direction for CASA, and by undertaking a review of CASA's funding arrangements to ensure the Authority was equipped to deal with new regulatory challenges; that CASA's Regulatory Reform Program be brought to a conclusion as quickly as possible to provide certainty to the industry, and to ensure CASA and the industry were ready to address future safety challenges; and that the Australian National Audit Office audit the Authority's implementation and administration of its Safety Management Systems approach.

CHAPTER 20

THE BLACK SATURDAY BUSHFIRES

7 FEBRUARY 2009

The Black Saturday bushfires were a series of apocalyptic blazes that burned across Victoria on – and for some weeks after – Saturday, 7 February 2009. As a result of the bushfires, 173 people died. It was the nation's largest loss of life from a bushfire event, and 414 people were injured. More than one million animals perished. Some 2030 homes were destroyed, displacing around 7560 people, and thousands more dwellings were damaged. More than 450 000 hectares of urban districts, rural fringe land, farm land and national park were scorched. The disaster cost $45 billion. Victorian Premier John Brumby said the fires were tantamount to 'hell on earth', while Prime Minister Kevin Rudd, visiting the scorched Yarra Valley on 8 February, described the firestorm as hell's fury unleashed, and continued, 'Many good people now lie dead. Many others lie injured. This is an appalling tragedy for Victoria but, because of that, it's an appalling tragedy for the nation. The nation grieves with Victoria tonight.' Victoria was shrouded by smoke and profound sadness.

Given the prevailing weather conditions, it would have been a miracle if Victoria's disastrous series of fires in February and March 2009 had not happened. Warnings of the fires to come were given, but proved of little value when it came to the ferocious crunch.

On 6 February, Victorians were warned by fire services, police and politicians that tomorrow, 7 February, would be the worst day for bushfires in the state's history, and instructed to take every precaution to save their lives and their property. A total fire ban was ordered, and 3582 firefighters put on red alert. Premier Brumby announced, 'It's just as bad a day as you can imagine and on top of that the state is just tinder-dry. People need to exercise real common sense tomorrow … It will be the worst day for bushfires in the history of the state.'

And so it proved.

As the Bureau of Meteorology, police and fire services had forecast, temperatures roared into the mid to high 40s, making it the hottest day in the state's history, and winds blew at a gale force 100 kilometres per hour. Humidity was low. Following a recent heat wave, and there having been no rain for many months, the bush was bone-dry.

The fires that sprang to life were ignited by bushland bursting into flames in the intense heat, by fallen power lines, sparks from machinery, discarded cigarettes – and by arsonists. A cool change at 5 p.m. that day brought no relief. In fact, the opposite. It summoned south-westerly winds in excess of 120 kilometres per hour, which turned the flanks of the fires into monster conflagrations that changed direction and burned with unimagined speed and ferocity towards towns whose residents were hoping they had been spared.

The seventy-eight townships attacked by the fires, and where there were fatalities, included Kinglake, Strathewen, Marysville, Flowerdale, Narbethong, Wandong, St Andrews, Koornalla, Callignee, Taggerty, Steels Creek and Humevale.

The inferno swept on at a frightening rate, jumping highways, whipped by the wind into a vast and deadly fireball which gained pace as it raced up the steep wooded hills in its path. At points in its rampage, the roaring fire was leaping 100 metres above the tree line. Anyone approaching within 300 metres of it was roasted by the radiating heat. The sky was black and scarlet, the colour of a bad bruise, and the air in the vicinity of the fires was chokingly acrid and burned the lungs of those who breathed it. Many of the victims perished in their homes, either caught by surprise or having made the decision to stay and fight. Others were incinerated in their cars after they bundled their loved ones, pets and prized possessions in and tried to speed to safety.

But back to noon on that terrible day, Black Saturday. The wind was blasting at more than 100 kilometres per hour and the temperature was recorded in places at 46 degrees. Fires ignited simultaneously. Power lines at Kilmore East in the Kinglake–Whittlesea district were knocked down by the gale, and the sparks that flew from the fallen power lines ignited the surrounding grasslands. Fanned by winds that were now 125 kilometres per hour, one monstrous blaze entered a pine forest, hurdled the Hume Highway, raced across the treetops – growing in intensity all the while – and made south-east towards Wandong and the surrounding district. At 12.30 p.m. the Horsham fire began, followed at around 2.50 p.m. by a bushfire that started in the Murrindindi Mill and which grew to terrifying proportions and burned parallel to the Kilmore East fire. By 4.20, the Kilmore East fire was laying waste to Strathewen. At that time, too, Narbethong was ablaze. Across the state, the fires numbered in the hundreds. It was 4.45 p.m. when the Kilmore East fire attacked Kinglake. The appalling number of lives it claimed – 122 – and the amount of destruction it wrought would not be known for days. At its height, smoke plumes from the Kilmore East fire soared 15 kilometres into the air.

At around 5 p.m. on 7 February, the north-westerly wind became a south-westerly, causing the Kilmore East and the Murrindindi Mill fires to merge. The united conflagration destroyed much of Flowerdale, and then linked with the Beechworth fire. This fire complex was the largest of the Black Saturday bushfires. It caused the deaths of 159 people – including those at Kinglake – burned 330 000 hectares of land and destroyed over 1800 houses.

Prime Minister Rudd announced that a federal-state emergency relief fund of $10 million had been established for those affected by the fires, and that those in need of immediate financial assistance were eligible for immediate Centrelink payments.

Firefighters, emergency services, police and the defence forces were engaged to battle the fires. By the time helicopters began ferrying the burned and smoke-affected to safety – as well as many who were injured in car crashes as they attempted to flee the flames on smoky roads – every hospital in the state was as ready as it could be to play its role in battling the disaster, and prepared to be inundated with burn victims. At 10 p.m. on Black Saturday, the official death toll was estimated at fourteen. That estimate turned out to be laughably, tragically low.

Flames from the Murrindindi Mill fire soared more than 100 metres into the sky as the fire crossed the Black Range. It turned to cinders 95 per cent of the houses of Narbethong and then, when the wind changed at 5 p.m., advanced on Marysville and did its worst. When it finally moved on, an eyewitness described the town as looking as if it had been 'nuked'. Reported a shattered Premier Brumby, 'There's no activity, there's no people, there's no buildings, there's no birds, there's no animals, everything's just gone. So the fatality rate will be very high.' It was. Some thirty-four died and all but fourteen of the town's 400 or so buildings were destroyed.

People died protecting their homes and livestock – sisters Penny and Melanie Chambers perished protecting their beloved horses at Kinglake – and sacrificed themselves so that loved ones might live. They died huddled in, and under, their homes; they died in paddocks and mills and factories and offices. Some were scalded to death after they sought refuge in swimming pools. Six were incinerated in their car while trying to escape from Kinglake. Arthur Enver, 57, mounted his Harley-Davidson motorcycle and sped out of Kinglake, but was overrun by the fireball and killed.

Among the deceased in the fires that assailed Kinglake West area were renowned ornithologist Richard Zann, his wife Eileen and daughter Eva, and the popular former television newsreader and children's talent show host Brian Naylor and his wife Moiree. Because their home was below a ridge, the Naylors were taken by surprise by the fire that advanced on them, literally riding the treetops. They had no hope of surviving, even though they had taken every precaution: in the yard of their property was firefighting equipment and a Mercedes-Benz four-wheel-drive vehicle; they had created firebreaks around their home with bulldozers. They fought to the end. 'Moiree and Bryan were the kind of people who might have died with their arms around each other,' said their friend, newsman John Sorrell. Another victim was the character actor Reg Evans, ubiquitous on Australian television and in films since the 1960s, appearing in TV's *Skippy*, *Prisoner*, *A Country Practice*, *Blue Heelers*, *Homicide* and *Number 96* as well as the movies *Mad Max*, *Gallipoli* and *Charlie and Boots*. Evans' partner, artist Angela Brunton, also perished.

Melanee Hermocilla, 23, her brother Jaeson, 21, and her boyfriend Greg Lloyd, 22, called Lloyd's family to say their final farewells when they realised that they would die at the home where they were house-sitting at Yarra Glen.

The nation was unstinting in its praise of the firefighters on the battleline, both professional and amateur, protecting what was dear to them, doing their utmost to the point of being badly burned and suffering exhaustion and asphyxiation, in the face of bushfires unprecedented in the destruction they wrought. They fought the conflagrations to the death, with bare hands, hoses, fire trucks, water-bombing helicopters. In newspapers and on TV, these ordinary citizens – eyes red and hollow, mouths grimly set and bodies blackened – brought the horror of what they faced in the Black Saturday fires into homes Australia-wide, and their experiences left a nation in profound shock and awe.

Eyewitnesses invariably spoke of the speed at which the fires travelled, of their terrible power and unbearable heat, of the ear-splitting roar that emanated from them. And they spoke of the way the fires plunged their towns into blackness though it was daylight. At night you could see the glow of a bushfire approaching from great distances, and still it was often too late to escape it.

The words of those caught in the maelstrom, spoken to each other, to firefighters, or to members of the press and electronic media, capture the devastation of those who uttered them. 'Holy Christ!' 'It's a holocaust.' 'God help us.' 'Trees are exploding in front of me.' 'All of a sudden we were in a raging inferno. There was coloured smoke and the noise was indescribable. It was terrifying.' 'Burned out cars are strewn along the road.' 'I prayed to the Lord to save my home ... but He didn't.' 'There are dead animals everywhere.' 'I saw a man disappear back into his home. He never came out. The house burned to the ground.' 'We only have the clothes on our back, but there's hundreds of people dead up there. Hundreds.' 'Don't bother donating televisions or fridges, we've got no home to put them in.' 'Mummy, am I going to be alive tomorrow?' 'I stared the devil in the face today.' 'Before we knew it, the fire was on top of us.' 'It's devastation, and people have seen horrific things today.' 'The fire was howling like every jet plane on the planet.' 'Darling… I'm alive!' 'There is only one building left standing in Marysville.' After the flames were put out at that benighted township, police prevented cars from entering because bodies remained strewn on the street.

Readers wept when they read of the plight of Marysville man Dan Walsh, as recounted to *Daily Telegraph* reporter Terry Brown:

> The 74-year-old looks to be one of the lucky ones, but his handshake is weak and his eyes are haunted. A car pulls up and he excuses himself, 'Got to talk to my son.'
>
> 'Mum's dead,' he tells his boy Michael, as bluntly as that. The young man drops to his knees by the roadside and sobs. Mr Walsh left his 73-year-old wife Marie at the plush Cumberland spa in the town's main street. They had gone there to sit out the worst, and by early evening the fire around there seemed over. 'I said, "It's gone now, but in case of fire, [go] out the door and down to the swimming pool area",' Mr Walsh says. 'I said I'd go back and see if I could save the house.'
>
> Wisps of smoke still rise around the yard and he walks in a daze putting them out. 'She must have gone further inside, thinking it was safer,' he says, trying to make sense where there is none. 'I'm just too shell-shocked to think. I'm just buggered.'

Prime Minister Rudd declared, 'As human beings we salute the extraordinary courage of all the emergency workers', and he could easily have been referring to the fireys who bundled nineteen people, including babies and toddlers, into the river at Murrindindi and hosed them under fire blankets as the flames devoured everything around them. Or to the volunteers of the Country Fire Authority (CFA), who fought the fires until they dropped from fatigue and smoke inhalation. Or to the RSPCA workers who cared for pets and livestock burned and injured in the blazes. Or to the Salvation Army officers who moved among the devastated and the grieving offering hugs and cool drinks and sandwiches. Or the counsellors who comforted those who had lost family, friends or property. Or to Peter Thorneycroft, 43, who, in T-shirt and thongs, climbed onto the roof of Kinglake's National Park Hotel with a garden hose and extinguished the embers that threatened to burn down the building in and around which 400 sheltered. Or to the so-called 'lunch ladies of Toolangi' in the Yarra Valley, who prepared hundreds of meals for the firefighters. Or to CFA volunteer 17-year-old Kelly Johnson, who joined other firefighters to train a high-powered hose on the CFA building in Kinglake where several hundred homeless people sheltered.

On 13 February it was announced that Australians and people from all over the world had pledged $76 million to a national appeal to aid the victims. Celebrities such as Russell Crowe, Orlando Bloom, Nicole Kidman, Hugh Jackman and Jimmy Barnes, as well as sports champions such as Shane Warne, manned phone lines to take note of the donors. The stars gave donations themselves. A CD, *Bushfire Aid* – the proceeds of which were all donated to the victims, and which featured songs by Bruce Springsteen, Billy Joel, Eurythmics, John Farnham and Jimmy Barnes – soared to the top of the charts.

Australians in huge numbers attended the 'National Day of Mourning, Together for Victoria' memorial services that were conducted across the nation on Sunday, 22 February, including those at Melbourne's Rod Laver Arena, Sydney Olympic Park and the forecourt of Sydney Opera House. The Rod Laver Arena memorial service was broadcast nationally on every television network.

Even as the fires still burned, the insurance industry received nearly 10 000 claims, totalling more than $1 billion. Rudd's successor as Prime Minister, Julia Gillard, hoped that, given the devastation, the industry would react to the claims 'sympathetically and quickly'. Mostly, it did.

Victorians – unlike people in other states, who were left in no doubt that they were expected to flee if their home seemed likely to go up in flames – had been encouraged to decide for themselves whether to stay and defend their homes or to evacuate them on 'code red or catastrophic fire risk' days.

Black Saturday changed all that. The Victorian government announced on 11 October 2009 that, in future, residents under threat would be advised that the safest course of action on a code red day was to flee at the earliest opportunity. Many of those who died in the Black Saturday fires had been killed while defending their property. Specific actions were recommended for each of the six fire danger categories: low to moderate; high; very high; severe; extreme; and code red (or catastrophic). The modification to policy would have received the blessing of Dan Walsh, who lost his wife Marie in the Marysville blaze. Said Walsh, a staunch supporter of community bushfire refuges:

> You only stay and defend if you have a chance of winning and in that situation, in that extreme heat, there's no chance of winning at all. The fire came down like a blast furnace. Telephone poles were spontaneously combusting 200 ft from the nearest burning thing. How do you stay and defend against that?

By the first week of March, when the fires were extinguished or expiring, the final toll of 173 people dead and 414 injured was known. More than a million birds and animals died as well, and millions more were badly burned.

Then, on 4 March, the merciful heavens opened – rain fell and the temperature dropped. The Kilmore East–Murrindindi fire complex, and many others, were contained at last. By mid-March, the fires were over. The pain never would be.

That pain was exacerbated when police confirmed that the Murrindindi Mill fire had been lit by arsonists, an act described by Prime Minister Rudd as 'mass murder'. When it emerged that many of the fires had been deliberately lit by fire bugs, no one argued with Rudd's assessment.

Incredibly, arsonists, having lit the deadly fires, returned to reignite them after they had been extinguished, condemning exhausted and singed firefighters to quell the flames once more. When he heard this, Premier Brumby broke down. His South Australian counterpart, Mike Rann, lambasted arsonists as 'terrorists within our nation, they are the enemy within and we have to be increasingly vigilant about them'. And an outraged New South Wales Premier Nathan Rees weighed in, saying anyone caught lighting fires should be swiftly and severely dealt with: 'This is not fun, this is not clever. This is something that can kill people.' Victoria's Deputy Police Commissioner Kieran Walsh warned arsonists that if they were caught they could be charged with murder.

One outraged resident of Churchill, Janice Michelsson, wrote a furious open letter to the arsonist who set the fires that turned her township to ash.

The letter was as angry as it was sad. It began 'You bastard', and continued:

> You are a fire terrorist. You are a murderer. You have taken my neighbours, my friends. You have taken my home. Do you hate people so much that you really want to see this misery. The damage you have caused is so great, I can't even bear to think of the horror my neighbours who sadly didn't make it were going through on Saturday. They would have thought, 'Oh my God, I'm trapped. Oh my God, I'm going to die.' In the end they were probably praying for death. What do you say to their families, friends and loved ones? As their neighbour, I am so incredibly sad. I will never see them and stop and say 'Hi' down at the supermarket. I will never wave to them when they drive past in their cars. I am lucky I got out of my home with just minutes to spare. I managed to save my cat and a photo album and that was all I could do before I was forced to run for my life.
>
> Yesterday I went back to where my home once stood. It was complete devastation. Today, I will go back with a crowbar and a sifter. My mum died not long ago and I kept many of her possessions. Today I will sift through the rubble and dust to look for her wedding ring.
>
> God bless the CFA and other emergency services. They risked their own lives to save ours and they are the true heroes who are still doing an amazing job.
>
> I heard a rumour yesterday [that] there was a person spotted riding a motorbike out in the pines with a can of petrol on the back. To him, and any arsonist, I would say, 'I'd like to get that can of petrol, pour it on you and light a match.' I've never wished harm on anyone before. Perhaps before that I would like to drive them to The Alfred Hospital in Melbourne, march them to the burns unit and have them explain to every single person there why they did what [they] did. If this person, or people, are ever caught, I never want to hear that they were suffering from a mental illness, from pyromania. They would get off with a slap on the wrist.

> This person, or people, knew exactly what they were doing. I am disgusted by you.

When one alleged arsonist was arrested and charged with setting fires, he received death threats.

The question incredulous and outraged people were demanding to know was, 'Who on earth could do such a thing?' Most of the arsonists arrested for starting a number of the Black Saturday fires fit in many ways the profile of an arsonist that was published in the August 2009 edition of *Psychotherapy in Australia*. Andrew Campbell's article was titled 'Bushfire Arsonists: Who Are They and Why Do They Do It?' and gave the psychological characteristics of the bushfire sociopath.

Traits typically exhibited by arsonists, found Campbell, included:

> deceitfulness, reckless disregard for the safety of others; consistent irresponsibility in occupational roles; lack of remorse and indifference to, or rationalisation for, hurting and mistreating others ... chronic emotional detachment, and absence of consequential thinking; dominated by primary process thinking and the pleasure principle at an infantile and regressed level but capable of manipulation and deception to avoid detection; alexithymia, a condition of impaired cognition and affect, and inability to express their feelings and thoughts in language, is evident in their confessions; poverty of affect and thought and concrete thinking reflect their incapacity to symbolise or empathise with human suffering; emotional life is dominated by negative feelings – boredom, contempt and devaluation of others; exhilaration and pleasure is felt through dominance; framed by early manifestations of psychopathology including cruelty to animals and fascination with fire; early signs of conduct disorder, persistent oppositional disorder, poor task completion, and in teenage years illicit drug use and anti-social conduct, and contact with law enforcement; may have obsession with sexual objects that have become fetishised, and collect pornography; fire-setting may

> be part of a paraphilia; likely sexual dysfunction and impotence; fantasised mastery achieved by fire-setting; inability to maintain relationships involving trust, love [and] reciprocity; tends to be misogynist with unresolved Oedipal conflict and enmeshment with mother; fears and resents dependence, and loss of an imagined loved object can initiate explosive rage in terms of fire-setting; recognised in local community as 'loners' and 'weirdos', with no web of social affiliations; fire is the compensatory and primary interest in their life.

Shockingly, many arsonists were employed as firefighters.

In the wake of the Black Saturday disaster, Victorian Police Commissioner Christine Nixon was empowered to form a task force comprising Victorian forensic police and their counterparts from other states and from overseas to assist in the identification of the victims, some of whom were burned beyond recognition. Investigations were also made into the causes of the fires and were able to confirm, repeatedly, that the answer was, as at Murrindindi, often arson. Looting also occurred, one of the most reprehensible cases involving thieves who lurked near burned houses, waiting until bodies had been removed, then moved in and pillaged the belongings of the deceased. Said Paul Lackas, whose brother Steve died, 'They are vultures.' At Kinglake, where a number of suspicious people were seen loitering near abandoned homes, a makeshift sign was erected: 'Looters Will Be Shot.'

A Royal Commission into the bushfires was established on 16 February 2009. It focused on the fires at Delburn, Bunyip, Kilmore East (including the Kinglake fire), Horsham, Coleraine, Pomborneit–Weerite, Churchill, Murrindindi (including the Marysville fire), Redesdale, Narre Warren, Upper Ferntree Gully, Bendigo and Beechworth–Mudgegonga. Its brief was to probe all aspects of the firefighting strategy, as well as the causes and chronology of the fires, and the damage done, and to assess how authorities from fire services, police, emergency services and governments performed in the crisis. The Black Saturday fires were now designated Australia's worst bushfire event – ahead of the Ash Wednesday fires in South Australia and Victoria in 1983, in which seventy-five people died, and Victoria's Black Friday fires in 1939, which killed seventy-one – and the eighth worst bushfires in recorded history.

On 31 July 2010, the four-volume, 900-page report of the Bushfires Royal Commission was released ... and while laudatory of the firefighters and emergency personnel on the ground, it was scathing in its criticism of some fire services and emergency management. The report said that poor leadership, a lack of warnings and government failures had left residents defenceless and at the mercy of the Black Saturday bushfires. The then Police Commissioner Nixon was criticised for her decision to visit her hairdresser and have a meal in a hotel on Black Saturday. 'Ms Nixon's approach to emergency co-ordination was inadequate,' noted the report. 'Ms Nixon herself acknowledged that leaving the integrated Emergency Co-ordination Centre and going home at about 6 p.m. on February 7 was an error of judgment.'

Also under fire were CFA chief Russell Rees and Ewan Waller, Chief Fire Officer of the Department of Sustainability and Environment. Both Rees and Waller, maintained the report, could have been expected to have done more in relation to 'warnings, supporting incident management teams and statewide planning'. Rees had made the error of relying on underlings to do these tasks. He had also not acted on the deadly south-westerly wind change on 7 February. Waller had not increased the warnings after the wind change, and could have lent more support to incident management teams. He had failed to pay attention to meteorological reports, and had delegated tasks to subordinates that he should have performed himself. The Emergency Services Minister Bob Cameron had made the decision to stay at his home in Bendigo on 7 February after being assured by fire authorities that they could cope. Hearing how serious the situation was at about 5.30 p.m., he decided to drive to the Integrated Emergency Control Centre in Melbourne, arriving around 8 p.m. While the Commission found that Cameron had done nothing wrong by remaining at home, they criticised him for not calling a state of emergency earlier in the day.

The Commissioners, Chairperson The Honourable Bernard Teague, AO, and Ronald McLeod, AM, and Susan Pascoe, AM, confirmed that 173 people died as a result of the fires: 119 in the Kilmore East fire, forty in the Murrundindi fire, eleven at Churchill, two at Beechworth–Mudgegonga, and one at Bendigo. The great majority died on 7 February. Wrote the Commissioners:

> The Commission heard many accounts from people who survived the 2009 bushfires, but it was only by examining the circumstances of the deaths that it could complete its investigation ... In particular, the examination of the circumstances of the deaths helped the Commission expand its knowledge of the way people understand and respond to bushfire. These inquiries also cast light on its consideration of matters such as planning and building regulation, the need for a broad range of safety options, and what makes a home defendable against bushfire.

CHAPTER 21

SHIPWRECK AT CHRISTMAS ISLAND

15 DECEMBER 2010

As Abdul Khaliq Fazal, President of the Afghan Australian Association of Victoria, would later sadly note, 'These people had committed no crime. They were coming for a better life to a place they thought would be paradise.' Instead, on the jagged limestone coast of Christmas Island, location of a burgeoning detention centre for asylum seekers, they found hell.

Somewhere between seventy and ninety Iraqis, Iranians and Kurds huddled on board the flimsy 16-metre wooden vessel as it approached Christmas Island – an Australian territory in the Indian Ocean some 2600 kilometres north-west of Perth and 360 kilometres south of Jakarta, capital of Indonesia – at dawn on 15 December 2010. The men, women and children were fleeing misery, war, oppression and poverty in their native lands. Most had weighed up the pros and cons of embarking on such a risky journey through treacherous seas via Indonesia, and – after further persuasion from rapacious people smugglers, who packed them onto the unseaworthy vessel later designated the SIEV 221 – decided that asylum in Australia was worth it.

Though numerous vessels transporting asylum seekers from such troubled lands as Sri Lanka, Iran, Afghanistan and Iraq had safely landed on Australian shores, the poor souls on this flimsy vessel were not so fortunate. Conditions were difficult. Driving rain had reduced visibility to less than 150 metres, the swell was pitching at 4 metres high, and the wind blew at 40 knots.

At around 6.30 a.m., while its navigators were trying to find a safe inlet on Christmas Island on which to land, the boat collided with the cliffs and rock shelves on the shoreline of aptly named Rocky Point at Flying Fish Cove, at the northern end of the island. The collision destroyed the power and steering of the vessel, rendering it unnavigable. It was now at the mercy of 3–4 metre waves and an onshore gale which, for more than an hour, smashed it again and again against the rocks, breaking the boat into pieces. Many asylum seekers were flung overboard and drowned. Others grasped flotsam and jetsam which was dashed onto rocks, with fatal results for those using them as life buoys.

Christmas Islanders – including around fifty members of the community and Customs and Border Patrol officers – rushed to the scene, but were largely powerless to help because of the huge seas and the razor-sharp rocks. They threw life jackets, surfboards and ropes at the floundering boat, to little avail. By the time rigid inflatable tenders from HMAS *Pirie* and ACV *Triton* arrived an hour or so later to assist the rescue efforts of the locals, it was too late for as many as forty refugees, perhaps more. (The exact number of those who died can never be known, for although forty-one asylum seekers were rescued and thirty bodies recovered from the sea, a number of bodies were never recovered.) The navy men were met with the terrible and never-to-be-forgotten sight of lifeless forms – including those of babies and children – bobbing pathetically in the tumultuous seas.

One man saved himself by making a mighty leap from the vessel and hanging onto rocks until he could be saved.

A witness who watched the tragedy unfold from the shore said he knew as soon as he saw the beleaguered vessel being pummelled against the rocks that 'it was obvious that someone was going to die. They were sitting out within metres of the cliff and they were all screaming, "Help us!" There were waves pounding into it and a lot of backwash, really bad weather.'

Recalled one Christmas Island resident who was standing on the cliff top, 'We saw people drowning who did get off the boat but unfortunately were hit against the limestone rocks. One person jumped off a piece of flotsam and [tried to reach] a naval rescue boat, but that ended in tragedy.'

One Christmas Islander told a reporter from Melbourne's *Herald Sun*, 'I went down to look and all I saw were people hanging on for dear life and the boat was being smashed against the rocks. It was horrible. They were screaming and yelling for help and falling into the ocean. We just felt so hopeless, there wasn't anything we could do.'

Said another onlooker, 'There was just debris and people everywhere in the water. The water conditions were horrific ... You couldn't blame this incident on anyone bar those who sent them.'

The government announced that it would conduct a criminal investigation into the shipwreck, under people-trafficking laws. The feeling of the nation was summed up by Allison Millcock, a contractor with the Shire of Christmas Island, who railed, 'These bastards who are bringing these boat people should be shot. They're criminals. They are absolute criminals.'

Answering criticism that the boat should have been intercepted by the Navy and Customs officials before it collided with the cliffs, officials insisted that the boat had approached Flying Fish Cove under cover of darkness, and by the time its presence was known it was being dashed against the rocks. The boat's dawn arrival had been 'a huge surprise'.

The survivors – who suffered a combination of immersion, bruising, abrasions or broken limbs – were treated on the island by doctors flown in on Royal Flying Doctor Service aircraft, and the flying doctors jetted three asylum seekers with severe head wounds and abdominal injuries to Perth hospitals after Western Australian Premier Colin Barnett offered the federal government all assistance. In the days after the calamity, forensic pathologists, Western Australian police and Australian Federal Police officers arrived on Christmas Island to identify victims.

On 19 December, a 'dignified, respectful' memorial service was organised by immigration officials and Islamic leaders at the island's Phosphate Hill for the known victims of the disaster: thirteen men, nine women, four children and four babies. It was the first ceremony of many. The survivors attended, still traumatised by the shipwreck and the grisly task of identifying the dead. Said Immigration Department spokesman Peter Richards:

> It is a very difficult time for the survivors but also for other people within the detention facilities. There are a number that we've identified, for example, that have relatives amongst [the deceased] … The issues around asylum and what eventually will happen with the survivors, including the orphans, is something that it's too early for us to speculate [on].

Federal Immigration Minister Bowen announced that counselling was being offered to asylum seekers in the Christmas Island facilities.

According to the federal government, the boat was the 126th to arrive in Australia in 2010, and some 2971 asylum seekers were being housed at the Christmas Island Detention Centre. (The Opposition took issue with figures, putting the numbers at 197 vessels and 5400 detainees respectively.)

Prime Minister Julia Gillard insisted that most Australians acknowledged the need to be sympathetic to the plight of those who put their lives at risk to start a new life in Australia. She called for a non-partisan political approach to the problem of increased numbers of creaky and dangerous vessels crammed to bursting with asylum seekers leaving trouble spots at the instigation of people smugglers and setting out for Australia. 'This has been a tragic event,' she said, 'and it will be some time before there is a full picture of what has happened. The government's focus and absolute priority is on rescue, recovery and treatment of the injured.'

Opposition Leader Tony Abbott spoke for many Australians angry at the hundreds of fatalities among asylum seekers: in April 2009, five Afghan refugees died when their boat blew up; in November that year, twelve Sri Lankans perished when their boat sank near the Cocos (Keeling) Islands; in May 2010, five Sri Lankan asylum seekers drowned; in October 2001, 353 asylum seekers perished when their vessel, the SIEV X, went down off Indonesia; and other boats have disappeared in heavy seas with the loss of all on board, numbers that cannot be known. Abbott blamed the government's relaxation of the restrictions implemented by the previous, Liberal, government. He pressed for a return to temporary protection visas, offshore processing at the Nauru Detention Centre and the option of turning boats around and sending them back to their country of origin if it was safe to do so. 'In the last five years of the Howard Government's life, we had three boats [arriving in Australia] a year, not three boats a week. Obviously there is far less capacity for tragedy if there are far fewer boats and far fewer people coming in them.'

When the decrepit vessel came to grief on the rocks at Christmas Island, the fate of asylum seekers coming to Australia had long been a pressing and controversial political issue. Vessels transporting asylum seekers began arriving on Christmas Island in the late 1980s, and the refugees were processed and detained before either being returned to their homeland or allowed to assimilate into Australian society. The island was the site of the notorious Tampa controversy in which the Howard Government refused to allow the Norwegian ship MV *Tampa* to unload its human cargo of 438 asylum seekers. The government's stand polarised opinion and laid the foundations for the fierce debate that ensues over the fate of asylum seekers who make it to Australian shores to this day.

There was another explosive incident in October 2001, when federal Liberal government ministers claimed that after a boat believed to be operated by people smugglers was intercepted by HMAS *Adelaide* 190 kilometres north of Christmas Island, asylum seekers on board had hurled their children into the ocean in an attempt to be rescued and gain passage to Australia, or in protest at being turned away. The claim was later proven false. It was theorised that it had been an attempt by the conservative, anti-asylum seeker politicians to galvanise public opinion against the arrival of refugees.

In another step to curb the arrival in Australia of asylum seekers – and, consequently, the burgeoning wealth of people smugglers who took payment from desperate refugees then herded them onto leaky boats navigated by incompetent seamen – the Howard Government passed legislation excising Christmas Island from Australia's migration zone, so preventing asylum seekers from automatically applying to the Australian government for refugee status. After being housed, treated and returned to health on Christmas Island in $400 million, 800-bed detention facilities there, the Royal Australian Navy would repatriate asylum seekers arriving on local shores to Nauru and Manus Island in Papua New Guinea for processing and for decisions to be made on their future. The new Rudd Government, on ousting the Liberals from power in 2007, opened discussions to deregister the Manus Island and Nauru centres and have all processing done at Christmas Island. The Gillard government remains allied to this decision.

The tragedy of 15 December 2010 continues to incite emotion. But, politics aside, what should never be forgotten, say those who witnessed the terrible events unfold, is the heroism of the rescuers. Said Harbour Master

Dave Robertson, 'The Navy and Customs acted swiftly and heroically in manoeuvring their inflatable boats in dangerous conditions. What they did to save that many people in those conditions was extraordinary. Those coxmen are heroes.'

An internal Australian Customs and Border Protection Service report into the tragedy was made public on 23 January 2011. It found that the Service had no way of knowing when SIEV 221 sailed from Indonesia, or when it would arrive at Christmas Island. The report also stated that Customs and Border Protection personnel had acted appropriately throughout the disaster, and deserved recognition for their deeds. Said CEO Michael Carmody:

> In putting their own lives at risk in extremely dangerous circumstances to rescue 41 people from the sea, the crews of HMAS *Pirie* and ACV *Triton* deserve our highest praise ... The material available to me has indicated that all persons involved have acted in accordance with policies, processes and procedures relevant to the exercise of their duties and, where there was not a specific policy, process or procedure in place due to the unprecedented nature of this tragic event, have acted appropriately and exercised good judgment.

The report recommended that, to avert further disasters, a land-based radar surveillance system be trialled and that extra safety and rescue equipment – such as life jackets which can be 'fired' through the air towards people in the sea some distance away – be stored at strategic locations. Radio equipment programmed to the same bandwidth would be installed at points around Christmas Island so those in trouble can communicate with the Service. The Australian Federal Police and the Department of Regional Australia would upgrade their Christmas Island ships.

While Prime Minister Gillard commended the actions of the Customs and Border Protection Service and its recommendations, Federal Attorney-General Robert McClelland said the review was no substitute for a more thorough inquiry being conducted by the West Australian coroner, and investigations by the Australian Federal Police and Western Australian police. The results of those inquiries have not been released at time of going to press.

Attorney-General McClelland defended the government's inability to track SIEV 221's voyage, saying, 'Intelligence is an imprecise science. All I can say is our agencies do their best. They are well resourced to do it, but given the clandestine nature of these criminal activities ... not each and every voyage will be identified.'

On the heels of the Customs and Border Protection Service's report, three Indonesian fishermen among the survivors of SIEV 221 were arrested and charged with people smuggling. The trio – aged 22, 32 and 60 – were charged with one count each of facilitating the bringing to Australia of a group of five or more persons, contrary to section 233C of the *Migration Act 1958*. On May 12 2011, Iranian-born Australian citizen Ali Khorram Heydarkhani, 40, who has been accused of masterminding the ill-fated voyage, was extradited from Indonesia where he was being held to Australia. He was scheduled to face a magistrate's trial in Perth in June.

CHAPTER 22

THE QUEENSLAND FLOODS

DECEMBER 2010 – JANUARY 2011

The great flood of 2010–11 was a disaster of Biblical proportions. The result of more than forty days and forty nights of torrential rain, which burst the banks of rivers and proved too much for dams, it turned three-quarters of Queensland into a vast and deadly lake.

In its history, Queensland has suffered horrific bushfires, droughts, floods and cyclones. Many Queenslanders have a propensity to mull over past disasters and argue – perhaps on the porch over a beer – just which was the biggest and baddest disaster, then marvel at the way the hardy locals survived and prevailed. These days, at least as far as floods are concerned, and despite the great floods of 1893 and 1974, there can be no further argument. The worst floods to befall Queensland were those that inundated central and southern Queensland in December 2010 and January 2011.

The floods were caused when the torrential rains of Tropical Cyclone Tasha coincided and combined with a La Niña event. As many as thirty-five people died, and at press time nine people were still unaccounted for. Tens of thousands of people were evacuated from their homes. Damages were estimated at more than $30 billion.

People and livestock, homes, cars, boats, trains, buses, trucks and bridges were simply swept away in the rush of brown water that reminded many of a monstrous chocolate milkshake. Up to 400 roads, including major highways, were rendered impassable, mines were flooded, railways closed, and towns on the northern coast were infested with snakes and crocodiles. At the flooding's height, three-quarters of the state – including the cities and towns of Brisbane, Ipswich, Toowoomba, Rockhampton, Emerald, Bundaberg and Dalby – was declared a disaster zone, as the Brisbane, Fitzroy, Burnett, Ballone, Condamine and Mary rivers and the dams along them broke their banks and burst, or were opened to release the gathering water. Queenslanders took the advice of Police Commissioner Bob Atkinson when he told them, 'We ask people not to panic. Stay calm and act wisely, and if you're in doubt, evacuate. Don't take any unnecessary risks.'

The rains fell and fell ... and the towns went under. In December, Chinchilla and Condamine were drowned. The residents of Theodore –

numbering around 300 – were airlifted to safety at evacuation centres when the Fitzroy River broke, many being plucked by helicopter from the roofs of their homes. On 29 December, 1200 Emerald residents were evacuated when the Nogoa River rose. By the next day it had reached a peak of around 16 metres. Rockhampton knew what was coming and precautions were taken. Nevertheless, by early January the town was underwater. The Burnett River flooded Bundaberg; 300 homes were evacuated. Chinchilla, Jericho, Dalby and Warwick went under and were isolated when the surrounding roads were cut off. The Condamine River reached a record high of 14.25 metres on 30 December, and the town of Condamine was consequently evacuated.

Television cameras captured James Perry, his wife Jenny Thorncraft and 9-year-old son Teddy perched on their car waving for help as the waters swirled around them. Mother and son were rescued by a helicopter which lowered a winch to them. The rescuers could not save James, who was swept away.

After 160 millimetres of rain teemed down on 9 and 10 January, flash floods struck Toowoomba. The two creeks – East and West creeks – that course through the centre of Toowoomba and converge to the north of the CBD smashed their banks on the afternoon of 10 January and a 3-metre wall of water rushed through the streets of the city, sweeping cars with it down Chalk Drive and James, Kitchener and Margaret streets at a rampaging velocity that destroyed buildings, trees and vehicles. Furniture, refrigerators, television sets and other items were swept from inundated stores and plunged down the streets, along with carcasses of drowned animals. A house on Russell Street was washed off its foundations and fell in a crumpled heap with a crack like thunder.

The flash flood claimed the lives of Donna Rice and her 13-year-old son Jordan, who died when their vehicle was swept away. Jordan and Donna Rice were tied with a rope to the roof of their car in Toowoomba's main street in an ultimately unsuccessful bid to thwart the floodwaters. Truck driver Warren McErlean came to rescue the boy. Jordan, who could not swim and was terrified of the water, nonetheless beseeched the truckie to first save his younger brother Blake, 10, which McErlean did. By the time he returned to rescue Jordan, he and his mother had been washed to their doom. Days later, when the details of their deaths became known, Jordan would come to epitomise the bravery and selflessness of Queenslanders in the floods.

Also on 10 January, flash floods roared into nearby Grantham, Helidon, Withcott and Murphys Creek. The bodies of Sandy and Steve Matthews, parents of four children, were recovered near their home at Murphys Bluff, near Toowoomba. The Matthews had assisted their family to evacuate the home before Sandy was trapped in the kitchen by a refrigerator that fell and blocked the door. Steve Matthews returned to help his wife, but as he was doing so a wall collapsed upon them and they were washed away.

In Grantham, east of Toowoomba, the bodies of nine townsfolk were recovered and some sixty-six were reported missing. Queensland Premier Anna Bligh said that Grantham had been swamped and destroyed by 'an inland tsunami'.

Amid the tragedy at Grantham, there was at least one happy ending. After searching for two days for his wife Natalie and their children without success, local man Norrie Blume was certain they had died. When Natalie finally contacted her husband – she and the kids had been rescued by police from the roiling waters and taken to Helidon, but she was unable to let Norrie know because there was no telephone communication – he collapsed with relief. 'I'm not going to lie – I blubbed and blubbed. There is no way to describe the relief,' Norrie told a reporter. He then reflected on his ruined town: 'It's like a bomb site – completely destroyed. I keep seeing house after house smashed up and thrown all over the place.'

Grantham, too, was the scene of extraordinary efforts by Ray Van Dijk and Daniel Moore to save their neighbours in a craft that resembled an Indian canoe and which cost Van Dijk a bargain $200 at a roadside stall. The pair paddled and pushed their boat in the chest-high water in the dark, the rain falling heavily all the while, calling out, 'Is anybody there?' and plucking those who called for help from the waters. Van Dijk and Moore saved dozens of people, depositing many of them on the increasingly congested roof of Van Dijk's submerged house. By the time they finished there was a crowd clustered high, if not dry. Said Moore, when lauded for his and his friend's bravery, 'We're not special. We just did what had to be done.'

In Toowoomba, traumatised and terrified residents told their stories to the converging media, including the Brisbane *Courier-Mail* and Sydney's *Daily Telegraph*. Reported bank worker Judith Grauer:

> You could see the water rushing at speed. It came up quickly and covered the roundabout. Then it started moving toward a row of parked cars along the street. The cars started to buckle under the stress. The water was absolutely tearing through the park, ripping out trees. Some people tried to move their cars but others just watched as the water washed them away ... I've never seen anything like it.

And Toowoomba local Penny Cowell:

> I saw tyres, wheelie bins, a water tank, a shipping container and a pedestrian footbridge swept away ... One car kept getting smashed against a power pole, eventually ripping off the back bumper. I saw a young woman sitting inside that car, but there was no way anyone could have got close enough to her to get her out.

A regional councillor in Grantham, Peter Friend, told reporters from the *Sydney Morning Herald* and AAP:

> There were people hanging onto the gutters of their houses, caught in trees, and an entire house that crashed over the railway line ... The pub was destroyed. It was unbelievable ... you just can't comprehend it until you're in the middle of it. [When Lockyer Creek broke its banks, the water] came straight down the highway in a big ball about 2 or 3 metres high and 2 kilometres wide. It took 15 minutes from when I saw it on the horizon to when it came roaring past. You could hear it. It had all sorts of debris – trees,

> wood, animals, parts of people's houses, sheds ... Houses were washed off their stumps.

People and wildlife dashed to what they hoped would prove to be higher, safer, ground.

At Gatton, Lockyer Creek rose to 18.92 metres, the highest level in recorded history.

Before the deluge, Queensland Labor Premier Anna Bligh was unpopular with the electorate and seemed certain to suffer a landslide defeat at the next election. But her cool aplomb, tirelessness and impressive grasp of the facts as she travelled the state – dispensing compassion and sound advice, speaking plainly without overblown rhetoric or offering false hope, shedding some tears along the way when she surveyed the damage – changed all that. She gave Queenslanders an inspiring, Churchillian performance in their darkest hour. The Premier, in rising to the occasion, found her way into the hearts of even staunch political opponents.

In Grantham – where people had died, sixty-odd folk were missing and homeless people were sleeping on their rooftops and in school halls – she said, 'Right now, we have every possible available resource deployed in this region to search for those people that we know are missing. This is going to be, I think, a very grim day, particularly for the people in that region, and a desperate hour here in Queensland.' Later, she declared, 'We have a grim and desperate situation ... It might be breaking our hearts at the moment, but it will not break our will.' And again, this time with her voice cracking with emotion:

> As we weep for what we have lost, and as we grieve for family and friends and we confront the challenge that is before us, I want us to remember who we are. We are Queenslanders. We are the people they breed tough north of the border. We're the ones that they knock down, and we get up again.

Teeming, ceaseless rain flooded the Lockyer Valley and when the deluge linked with the torrents that continued to fall over south-east Queensland,

Brisbane found itself in terrible danger. The waters rushed into the already swollen-to-bursting Brisbane River and into the catchment of the Wivenhoe Dam, which, ironically, had been constructed to stop a repeat of the devastation wrought by the 1974 floods. Authorities had to release water from the dam so it would not overflow, or burst with the pressure of the water it was retaining. The overflow, supplemented by enormous amounts of uncontrolled water from the Bremer River and Lockyer Creek, headed down the Brisbane River towards Brisbane which, to make matters even worse, was due for a king tide.

The Brisbane CBD and suburbs – especially Fortitude Valley, St Lucia, Graceville, Rockville, New Farm and West End, Bellbowrie, Moggill, Karana Downs and Pullenvale – were inundated on 12 January, when the Brisbane River, which simply could not cope with the onrush of water, broke its banks. Said Brisbane Lord Mayor Campbell Newman as the torrent approached, 'Today is very significant, tomorrow is bad, and Thursday is going to be devastating ... who knows what happens then on Friday.' He was right to be deeply concerned.

There were incredible sights as the raging waters turned the modern city with its wide thoroughfares, historic buildings, picturesque parks, shopping precincts and office towers into a wet and wild waterworld. On 13 January, the Brisbane River hit its highest level of 4.46 metres. Around 20 000 homes and businesses were inundated. Millions of dollars worth of leisure and fishing boats were picked up by the floods and many were smashed into splinters on the river banks. The Brisbane Riverwalk – a floating walkway linking the city with nearby suburbs – was smashed by the waters, a 310-metre section breaking off and floating at 12 knots down the river. It would have crashed into the structural supports of the Story Bridge were it not for the brave efforts of tugboat captain Doug Hislop and fellow skipper Peter Fenton, who piloted their tugs to manoeuvre the monster chunk of debris safely under the bridge. Suncorp Stadium, home ground of the Brisbane Broncos rugby league team, was awash. On the field the water was 2 metres deep, rising as high as the fourth row of seats, and leading some to wonder if the ground would now be better suited to water polo or swimming events.

Aside from Grantham, the working-class city of Ipswich, 34 kilometres south-west of Brisbane, was worst hit. There, the Bremer River rose to an incredible 19.4 metres. Residential streets and the business district were metres underwater. A third of the city was submerged. Bull sharks swam through the streets of the Ipswich suburbs of Gailes and Goodna.

Gympie was bisected by the floodwaters from the Mary River – normally around 20 metres wide, it now neared 600 metres in breadth in some sections – with scores of homes and shops underwater as the water rose to 1.5 metres in the central parts of town. Fish were seen swimming in the murky water that rose to a metre in the front bar of the Royal Hotel.

Prime Minister Julia Gillard addressed those besieged by the floods: 'There are people who are frightened, people desperately waiting for news of loved ones. My thoughts and my sympathies are now with you.' As were those of Opposition Leader Tony Abbott, who assured the suffering that 'the thoughts and prayers of all Australians will be with the families of those who have died and those who are missing'. Donations from the public and corporations literally flooded in from Australia and overseas to the Premier's Disaster Relief Appeal (which would raise well over $55 million) and to the St Vincent de Paul Flood Appeal, the Red Cross Disaster Relief and Recovery Appeal and the Salvation Army.

English cricket champion Kevin Pietersen took time out from helping his team-mates wallop the Aussies in the Ashes series to auction his shirt and bat, all proceeds going to flood victims. For good measure, the man Australian crowds love to hate threw in two tickets to the Australia–England one-day international played in Perth on 6 February, flights from anywhere in the world and two nights' luxury accommodation to the highest bidder. Other sports stars lent a hand, such as Socceroo Tim Cahill, who offered a 'Tim Cahill Experience' in which 'two people get to bid for a chance to sit in my box personally from anywhere in the world and watch an Everton game, have some dinner, watch a training session, have a signed pair of boots and a jersey.' Musicians – including international stars Foo Fighters and Jimmy Buffett, and local artists Leo Sayer, The Choirboys, Christine Anu and Daryl Braithwaite – played and donated the money they earned to the sodden and needy.

The Nine Network broadcast the 'Flood Relief Appeal: Australia Unites' telethon, which raised more than $10 million. At the Twenty20 cricket match between Australia and England on 12 January the players donated their match payments and the crowd kicked in $28,450, throwing their coins, notes and cheques into buckets and blankets carried around the ground by the cricketers. There was a Rally for Relief tennis match at Melbourne's Rod Laver Arena, attended by 15 000 who came to see Roger Federer, Rafael Nadal, Lleyton Hewitt, Novak Djokovic and Andy Roddick play for the cause. And on 27 January, Parramatta Stadium in western Sydney was packed for the Legends of Origin rugby league match, in which champions of yesteryear defied age, burgeoning weight, aching joints and brittle bones to strap on their boots one more time for a State of Origin game. The match – which was played with no quarter asked or offered – raised $380 000 for the flood victims.

On 19 January, Jordan and Donna Rice were laid to rest in the one grave in matching white coffins, the son's resting on top of the mother's to signify that he was safe in her keeping. The nation joined their family and friends in farewelling the little hero and his mother. Cat Stevens' 'Father and Son' and Eric Clapton's 'Tears in Heaven' were played as the coffins were lowered. In his eulogy, Jordan's brother Chris, 22, spoke to Jordan, whose nickname was 'Weedsy':

> You were so shy, always hanging off Mum. You were petrified of water, heights and even the dark. How wrong was I. Here you go losing your life from one of your biggest fears to save your little brother. You made me so proud. What you did took heart, courage and love. You're my little hero. I love you, Weedsy. You will always be missed, mate, but I take comfort in the fact that you've got Mum there with you, taking care of you.

There was scarcely a dry eye at the service, or in the land, after Chris spoke. Then John Tyson – Jordan's father and Donna's husband – stepped up. 'The fire in my heart will continue to burn until my time comes to join them ... God speed, my little angels.'

When the waters receded, leaving debris, mud, broken lives and shattered dreams in their wake, Premier Bligh remained indomitable. 'The task before us is a reconstruction task of post-war proportions,' she said, as tradespeople, demolition and construction workers from Queensland and all over Australia prepared to roll up their sleeves. 'That is how we are seeing it and that is the sort of steely determination that it will require.'

Amid the camaraderie and volunteerism (some 55 000 citizens with buckets, shovels, brooms and gumboots, dubbed an 'army of angels', pitched in to mop up), there was a discordant note when some insurance companies refused to pay out on policies, claiming that certain people were covered for damage caused by rain, but not by rivers breaking their banks. The vast mop-up and rebuild would be conducted in tandem with a Judicial Inquiry, which would investigate the floods and probe how early warning of the impending disaster in such towns as Grantham were not acted upon.

At time of going to press, the drying out and the reconstruction of Queensland was gathering pace. The clean-up is expected to account for much of any hoped-for 2013 federal government budget surplus. The Queensland Reconstruction Authority would decide whether – and which – suburbs should be rebuilt and flood-proofed to avert such disasters in future.

REFERENCES

1 The Wreck of the *Dunbar*

ABC Premium News, 19 August 2007. *Daily Telegraph*, 25 August 2001; 20 August 2007. *Newsletter of the AIMA*, December 2007. *Signals*, March–May 2001; June–August 2007. *Sydney Morning Herald*, 18, 22, 24, 25, 26, 27, 28 August 1857; 16 August 1933; 7 June 1980; 18 August 2007

Australian National Maritime Museum and State Records, New South Wales

Migration Heritage Centre, 'Dunbar Shipwreck Collection' www.migrationheritage.nsw.gov.au/exhibition/objectsthroughtime/dunbar/

NSW Heritage Branch, 'The Ship Dunbar – New South Wales's Worst Shipping Tragedy' www.heritage.nsw.gov.au/maritime/wrk_dunbar.htm

'Shipwrecks' www.abc.net.au/ backyard/shipwrecks/

State Library of Victoria, *A Narrative of the Melancholy Wreck of the Dunbar*

2 Cyclone Mahina's Trail of Destruction

Australian Journal of Emergency Management, Autumn 2000. *Brisbane Courier*, 7, 8, 9, 10, 11, 13, 14, 15, 16, 17, 18, 20, 21, 22 March 1899. *Northern Territory Times*, 17, 31 March 1899. *Royal Historical Society of Queensland Journal*, February 2001. *Sydney Morning Herald*, 11, 13, 14, 15, 16, 17, 18, 20, 21 March 1899; 26 December 1974. *Torres News*, 17 November 2009.

Bureau of Meteorology, correspondence

Bureau of Meteorology website, www.bom.gov.au 'The Bathurst Bay Hurricane and Associated Storm Surge'

The Pearling Disaster 1899: A Memorial ('Outridge Booklet')

'They Called the Wind Mahina' www.afloat.com.au/afloat-magazine/2009/august-2009/They_called_the_wind_Mahina

www.wordiq.com (definition of storm surge)

3 The Spanish Flu Pandemic

Australian Cultural History, Vol. 16, 1997–98. *Brisbane Courier*, 26 October 1918; 4, 26 November 1918; 31 January 1919; 26 February 1919; 5 March 1919; 8, 23, 29 May 1919; 16, 23 June 1919; 17, 29 July 1919; 1, 4, 10, 12, 19, 22 August 1919; 5 September 1919. *Illawarra Mercury*, 30 May 2009. *Newcastle Herald*, 20 April 2006. *Northern Territory Times*, 12 April 1919. *Sydney Morning Herald*, 24 October 1918; 6, 18, 23 November 1918; 21, 25, 27, 28, 31 January 1919; 3, 4, 11, 21 February 1919; 1, 3, 12, 21, 27, 28 March 1919; 1, 7, 8, 10, 11, 14, 15, 16, 24, 25 April 1919; 2, 16 May 1919; 3, 7, 14, 16, 18, 20, 21 June 1919; 10, 29 July 1919; 19 August 1919. *Advertiser*, 28, 30 November 1918; 9, 23, 27, 29, 30 January 1919; 11 February 1919; 21 March 1919; 17 May 1919; 7, 14, 19 August 1919; 15 October 1919; 26 November 1919. *Argus*, 18, 25 November 1918; 2 December 1918; 8 March 1919; 1, 5, 8, 16 April 1919; 6, 9 May 1919; 2, 9, 28 June 1919; 4, 9, 15 July; 6, 11, 13, 18, 21, 30 August 1919; 16 September 1919. *Footprints*, December 2005. *Health and History*, Vol. 2, No. 1, 2000. *Mercury*, 29 January 1919; 8, 18 February 1919; 17 March 1919; 19 April 1919; 2, 30 June 1919; 1, 7, 9 July 1919; 1, 14, 16, 20, 21, 23 August 1919; 16, 26 September 1919. *Queenslander*, 30 November 1918; 1 February 1919; 22 March 1919; 10, 31 May 1919; 26 July 1919. *Teacher*, April 2009. *West Australian*, 27, 30 January 1919; 4 February 1919; 28 March 1919; 1, 15, 26 April 1919; 1 May 1919; 9, 10, 12, 17, 19 June 1919; 25 August 1919; 6 October 1919. *Western Argus*, 10 September 1918; 22 October 1918; 7 January 1919; 4 February 1919; 20 May 1919; 17 June 1919; 26 August 1919

Australian Department of Health and Ageing, 'Pandemic Influenza', 1918

'The 1918–19 Flu Pandemic in Australia' www.stanford.edu/group/virus/uda/

'Goody Two Shoes – Pantomime, 1919' www.hat-archive.com

'How Australia Prevented the Devastating 1918–19 Spanish Influenza', Macquarie University News www.fightflu.com.au
'The Influenza Pandemic of 1918' http://virus.stanford.edu/uda/
Howard Phillips and David Killingray (eds), *The Spanish Influenza Pandemic of 1918–19: New Perspectives,* Routledge, 2001

4 The Mount Mulligan Mine Explosion

Australian, 5 May 2008. *Brisbane Courier,* 20, 21, 22, 23, 24, 26, 27, 28, 29, 30 September 1921; 1, 3, 4, 5, 6, 7, 8, 10, 11, 12, 13, 15, 17, 18, 19, 21, 22, 25, 26, 27, 28, 31 October 1921; 1, 5, 8, 10, 11, 14, 19 November 1921; 3, 13, 31 December 1921; 7, 13 January 1922; 11, 14 February 1922; 22 March 1922; 13, 14, 25 July 1922; 20 October 1922; 15 June 1923; 18 February 1924; 8, 13, 15 October 1924. *Labour History,* No. 40, May 1981. *Mining Advocate,* October 2008. *Sun-Herald,* 20 September 2009
Community and Public Sector Union, 'National Review into Model Occupational Health and Safety Laws', 2008
'History of Mount Mulligan' www.athertontablelands.com.au/pages/history-of-mt-mulligan/
Monument Australia, 'The Day the Devil Wept', Mount Mulligan Cemetery www.monumentaustralia.org.au
Mount Mulligan Cemetery http://interment.net
Queensland Historical Atlas, 'Mount Mulligan Disaster, 1921' www.qhatlas.com.au/content/coal

5 The Sinking of the *Greycliffe*

Daily Telegraph News Pictorial, 4, 5, 7, 8, 9, 10, 11, 12, 14, 15, 16, 17, 18, 19, 21, 22, 23, 24, 25, 26 November 1927. *Daily Telegraph Sunday Pictorial,* 6, 13 November 1927. *Sydney Morning Herald,* 7, 8, 10, 12, 14, 15, 16, 17, 18, 19, 21, 22, 23, 24, 25, 26 November 1927; 29, 30, 31 December 1927; 4, 5, 6, 7, 9, 10, 11, 12, 13, 14, 17, 18, 19, 20, 21, 24, 25, 26, 28 January 1928; 1, 2, 3, 4, 8, 10, 24, 29 February 1928; 13 March 1928; 12, 14, 19 April 1928; 27 October 1928; 18, 20 March 1930; 8, 15 April 1930; 3 May 1930; 2, 29 July 1930; 18 February 1931; 27 October 1931; 15 February 1934; 23 August 1934; 3 November 1937; 5 December 2003
Steve Brew, *Greycliffe – Stolen Lives,* Navarine Publishing, 2003
Facebook, Greycliffe disaster
'Shipwrecks of Port Jackson and the Heads' http://oceans1.customer.netspace.net.au/portjackson-wrecks.html
'The 1927 Tahiti–Greycliffe Disaster' www.policensw.com/info/history/tahiti.html

6 The Tasmanian Floods

Argus, 18 October 1929. *Mercury,* 6, 8, 9, 10, 11, 12, 13, 15, 16, 17, 18, 19, 20, 22, 23, 24, 25, 26, 27, 29, 30 April 1929; 2 May 1929. *Sydney Morning Herald,* 13 January 1931; 8 February 2004
'Briseis Dam' www.economypoint.org/b/briseis-dam.html
Bureau of Meteorology Northern Tasmania, April 1929
Centre for Tasmanian Historical Studies, *Companion to Tasmanian History, 2006*
Department of Primary Industries, Water and Environment, 'Hydrological Analysis of the Ringarooma Catchment'

7 The Great Melbourne Storm

Age, 2 September 2003. *Argus,* 1, 3, 4, 5, 6, 13, 14, 15 December 1934; 24, 31 January 1935; 18 September 1935
Bureau of Meteorology, 'The December 1934 Floods in Melbourne' www.bom.gov.au/lam/climate/levelthree/c20thc/flood4.htm
R.N. Chenoweth, *Canoe Sport in Australia,* Australian Canoe Federation, 1949
City of Kingston, Kingston Historical Website, 'Blowing a Storm in 1934' http://localhistory.kingston.vic.gov.au
'Floods and drainage' eMelbourne
SES, 'Flood Reflections – Melbourne 1934' www.ses.vic.gov.au

8 The Broome Cyclone

West Australian, 28, 29, 30 March 1935; 1, 2, 3, 4, 6, 25 April 1935; 11 May 1935; 11 April 1936
Broome history www.broome.com.au

9 Bondi's Black Sunday

Argus, 7, 8, 26 February 1938. *Brisbane Times,* 2 August 2009. *Canberra Times,* 7, 22 February 1938; 10 March 1938. *Daily Telegraph,* 7, 8 February 1938; 19 May 2002; 9 December 2002; 21 February 2007; 6 February 2008. *Medical Journal of Australia,* 5 June 2006. *Sunday Herald,* 6 January 1952. *Sun-Herald,* 13 May 2001. *Sydney Morning Herald,* 7, 8, 9, 15, 16, 17, 26 February 1938; 2, 23 March 1938; 7 April 1938; 12 November 1946; 14 May 2001; 28 January 2002; 23 February 2005; 7 September 2007

ABC TV, *Dimensions in Time,* 13 May 2002

ABC TV, *7.30 Report,* 26 September 2006

Australian Bureau of Statistics, 'Surf Life Saving – An Australian Icon in Transition' www.abs.gov.au

Bondi Surf Club Hall of Fame Members

Mark D. and Laila E., 'Scratching Sydney's Surface', 22 January 2010 http://scratchingsydneyssurface.wordpress.com/

Encyclopedia of Australia, Aub Laidlaw

Surf Life Saving Sydney, excerpted from 'Black Sunday – Bondi 1938', *Surfline,* October 1982 www.surflifesavingsydney.com.au/Lifesaving-and-Education/Rescue-Methods/

Waverley Library, *Bondi's Black Sunday,* published by Waverley Library from sources within the Local History Collection

10 The TAA Fokker Friendship Disaster

ABC Premium News, 10 June 2004; 9 December 2009; 10 June 2010. *Age,* 26 November 1999. *Australian,* 26 May 2010. *Christian Today,* 14 June 2010. *Courier Mail,* 8 June 2009. *Daily Mercury,* 9, 11 June 2010. *Herald Sun,* 19 November 2000. *In Focus,* May 2010. *Morning Bulletin,* 10 June 2010. *Sun Herald,* 12, 19 June 1960. *Sydney Morning Herald,* 11, 13, 14, 15, 16, 17, 18, 20, 21, 22, 28 June 1960; 3, 4, 5, 6, 7, 8, 11, 12, 13, 18, 19, 20, 21, 22, 26, 27, 28 October 1960; 12, 14 December 1960; 10 June 1961

Australian Mooney Pilots Association, 'Worst Aussie Disaster', 21 December 2009 http://mooney.org.au/forum/viewtopic.php?f=10&r=362

Aviation Safety Network, 'Fokker Friendship Crash', 10 June 1960 http://aviation-safety.net/database/record.php?id=19600610-1

11 The Collapse of the West Gate Bridge

Sun Herald, 18 October 1970; 8 August 1971. *Sydney Morning Herald,* 16, 17, 19, 20, 21, 22, 24, 27, 29 October 1970; 3, 4, 5, 6, 7, 10, 11, 12, 13, 14, 18, 19, 21, 24, 25, 27, 28 November 1970; 1, 2, 3, 5, December 1970; 2, 4 January 1971; 3, 4, 5, 11, 12, 16, 17, 18, 23, 24, 26 February 1971; 2, 3, 4, 5, 11, 12, 13, 18, 26 March 1971; 1, 8, 27 April 1971; 8 May 1971; 3, 4, 5, 8, 9, 10, 16 June 1971; 4, 6, 9, 19 August 1971; 6, 11 September 1971; 6 November 1971; 22 December 1971; 16 February 1972; 17 March 1972; 18, 19, 26 April 1972; 29 June 1972; 4 July 1972; 3 August 1972; 24 October 1972; 23 November 1972; 8 December 1972; 2 February 1977; 31 May 1978; 1 June 1978; 16 November 1978; 14 August 1979

Architecture Australia, West Gate Bridge Memorial Park

Arnold Earnshaw, *Remember When ... Two Decades of Memorable Events and Colourful Personalities,* Angus & Robertson, 1984

Public Record Office Victoria, 'Disaster at West Gate'

'The West Gate Bridge and Pat Preston' www.westgatebridge.org/patpreston.html

Worksafe Australia, 'Collapse of the West Gate Bridge'

www.westgatebridge.org

12 Cyclone Tracy

Bulletin, 27 December 1995. *Australian Journal of Emergency Management,* August 2006; November 2008. *Australian Women's Weekly,* 15, 22 January 1975. *Issues,* Vol. 78, March 2007. *Journal of Australian Studies,* 1 September 2000. *Journal of Northern Territory History,* No. 10, 1999. *Sun-Herald,* 29 December 1974; 5, 12, 19 January 1975; 9 February 1975; 8 June 1975; 9 October 1983. *Sydney Morning Herald,* 26, 27, 28, 30, 31 December 1974; 1, 2, 3, 4, 6, 7, 8, 9, 10, 11, 13, 14, 15, 17, 18, 20, 23, 24, 28, 29, 30, 31 January 1975; 1, 3, 7, 8, 9, 12, 13, 14, 19, 22, 25, 26, 27, 28 February 1975; 7, 8, 10, 13, 15, 26,

31 March 1975; 1, 3, 10, 12, 17, 19 April 1975; 24, 27 May 1975; 2, 6, 14, 21 June 1975; 8, 9, 11 July 1975; 24, 26 December 1975; 6 May 1983; 24 December 1985; 19 November 1988; 16 November 1994; 24 December 1994

ABC Online, 'The Big Blow of Cyclone Tracy, 30 Years On', 1 December 2004 www.abc.net.au/nt/stories/s1255740.htm

Arnold Earnshaw, *Remember When ... Two Decades of Memorable Events and Colourful Personalities, Angus & Robertson, 1984*

Bureau of Meteorology, 'Cyclone Tracy, Christmas 1974' www.bom.gov.au

Gil Jennex, 'Cyclone Tracey [sic], Darwin, 1974 – An Experience', 23 March 2007 http://jennex.id.au/cyclone_tracey

Northern Territory National Library, 'Cyclone Tracy'

13 The Granville Train Smash

Australian Women's Weekly, 2 February 1977. *Daily Telegraph,* 19 January 2010. *Sydney Morning Herald,* 19, 20, 21, 22, 23, 24, 25, 27 January 1977; 2, 18, 22, 23, 24, 25 February 1977; 1, 2, 3, 4, 9, 10, 11, 12, 15, 16, 17, 18, 23, 24, 25, 26, 29, 30, 31 March 1977; 1, 5, 6, 9, 15 April 1977; 3, 24, 31 May 1977; 1, 2, 3, 10, 12 June 1977; 27 September 1977; 15 January 1978; 6, 30 June 1981; 11, 12 July 1981; 5 September 1981; 18 January 1982; 4 February 1982; 23 February 1985; 20 February 1986; 11, 17 January 1987; 4 October 1987; 17 December 1987; 17 January 1988; 6 February 1988; 18 January 1990; 19 January 1995; 18 January 2010

Arnold Earnshaw, *Remember When ... Two Decades of Memorable Events and Colourful Personalities,* Angus & Robertson, 1984

'A Bridge Too Far ... Down' www.bikeme.tv

Barry O'Farrell MP, speech given on 18 January 2009 to John Hennessy and members of the Granville Memorial Trust, commemorating the thirty-second anniversary of the Granville train disaster

'Commuter Train Wrecked' www.danger-ahead.railfan.net

Granville Historical Society, 'Granville Rail Disaster' www.granvillehistorical.org.au

Ken Howard, 'Granville Train Disaster' www.granvilletraindisaster.com/

NSW Coroner, *Coroner's Finding into the Granville Train Crash*

NSW Fire Brigades, 'Granville Train Disaster', 18 January 1977

14 The Alice Springs Balloon Plunge

Northern Territory News, 25 August 2000; 23 October 2003. *Seattle Times,* 2 December 1992. *Sun-Herald,* 3 December 1989; 26 August 1990. *Sydney Morning Herald,* 14, 15, 16 August 1989; 12 October 1989; 29 November 1989; 15, 17, 25, 27 August 1990; 1, 3 December 1992

Supreme Court of the Northern Territory, No. 51/1990, 12 November 1992, *The Queen v Michael Winston Sandby,* ruling on the voir dire; No. CA8/1992, 24–27 May 1993, *Michael Winston Sanby v R,* appeal

15 The Newcastle Earthquake

ABC Premium News, 28 December 2009. *Australian Journal of Emergency Management,* Vol. 10, No. 4, Summer 1995–1996. *Macedon Digest,* Vol. 5, No. 1, 1990. *Maitland Mercury,* 2, 3 January 1990. *Newcastle Herald,* 30 December 1989; 1, 3, 4, 15, 23, 30 January 1990; 1, 6 February 1990; 6 February 1990; 4 April 1990; 28 December 1994; 12, 28, 29 December 2009. *Sun-Herald,* 31 December 1989; 7, 21 January 1990. *Sydney Morning Herald,* 29, 30 December 1989; 1, 2, 3, 4, 5, 6, 8, 9, 10, 11, 13, 18, 20 January 1990; 9 January 2007

Australian Bureau of Statistics, *2008 Yearbook,* 'Natural Disasters in Australia'

16 The Boondall Bus Crash

Courier-Mail, 25, 26, 27, 29, 31 October 1994. *Sydney Morning Herald,* 25 October 1994

17 Landslide at Thredbo

AAP General News, 15 April 2002. *Age,* 8 August 1997; 30 June 2000; 30 July 2002. *Australian,* 21 July 2007. *Australian Journalism Review,* Vol. 20, No. 2, December 1998. *Australian Journal of Emergency Management,* Autumn 1998; Autumn 1999; Spring 1999; Summer 2001–2002.

Australian Women's Weekly, 1 August 2007. *Bulletin with Newsweek,* 12 August 1997. *Daily Telegraph,* 31 July 1997; 1, 2, 3, 4, 5, 6, 7, 8, 9, 10 August 1997; 18 October 2001; 31 July 2007. *Eastern Courier,* 18 November 2009. *Herald Sun,* 12 March 2001; 17 November 2001; 10 March 2002; 30 July 2007. *Sun-Herald,* 14 April 2002. *Sydney Morning Herald,* 12 March 2001; 3 December 2004. *Times,* 28 January 2007

ABC Radio National, *PM,* 29 June 2000

ABC TV, *7.30 Report,* 29 June 2000

Derrick Hand, Coroner, 29 June 2000, Report of the Inquest into the Deaths Arising from the Thredbo Landslide (on CD-ROM)

Roger D. Harris, 'Medical Log: Forward Command Thredbo' (1997) *Medical Journal of Australia* www.mja.com.au/public/issues/xmas/harris/harris.html

Parliament of New South Wales, Hansard transcripts, 17 September 1997

18 The Sydney Hailstorm

Australian Journal of Emergency Management, Summer 1999–2000. *Daily Telegraph,* 15, 16, 17, 19, 20, 21, 22, 29 April 1999; 27 June 1999. *Issues,* Vol. 78, March 2007. *Sunday Telegraph,* 18 April 1999

19 The Lockhart River Plane Crash

AAP Australian National News, 2 March 2007; 4, 5 April 2007; 21 May 2007; 4, 5, 7, 8, 18, 21, 26 June 2007; 5, 6 July 2007. ABC Premium News, 3, 7 June 2005; 31 August 2006; 5, 17 April 2007; 9 May 2007; 18 August 2007; 29 June 2009. *Australian,* 13 May 2005; 17 December 2005; 25 January 2006; 9 May 2007; 17 August 2007; 5 June 2008. *Cairns Post,* 10, 11, 12, 13, 28 May 2005; 14 June 2005; 21 October 2005; 4 November 2005; 16 December 2005; 8 May 2006; 4 June 2006; 15 August 2006; 1 September 2006; 6 December 2006; 5 April 2007; 5, 6, 7, 9, 20, 27 June 2007; 27 June 2008; 20 November 2009. *Courier-Mail,* 9, 10, 11, 12, 14–15, 21 May 2005; 4, 5, 23 April 2007; 6, 23, 28 June 2007; 4 July 2007; 18 August 2007; 16 June 2008; 3 July 2008; 4 October 2008. *Daily Telegraph,* 8, 9, 12, 13 May 2005; 26 June 2007. *Gold Coast Bulletin,* 14, 31 May 2005. *Sunday Mail,* 8 May 2005; 7 May 2006. *Sydney Morning Herald,* 8 May 2005. *Townsville Bulletin,* 11, 23 May 2005; 4 July 2005; 17, 23 December 2005; 22 May 2007; 7, 21, 29 June 2007; 6 July 2007; 5 November 2007; 4 March 2009. *Weekend Post,* 13 February 2010

ATSB Transport Safety Investigation Report and Appendices (on CD-ROM)

Queensland State Coroner, Finding of Inquest (on CD-ROM)

20 The Black Saturday Bushfires

Australasian Parks & Leisure, Autumn 2010. *Australian and New Zealand Journal of Public Health,* Vol. 33, No. 2, 2009. *Australian Forestry,* Victorian Fires: Retrospective and Prospective, Vol. 72, No. 3, 2009. *Australian Journalism Review,* December 2009. *Big Issue,* November 2009. *Building Economist,* March 2009. *Chain Reaction,* March 2010. *Company Director,* June 2009

Daily Telegraph, 9, 10, 11, 12, 13, 14, 16, 17, 18, 19, 21 February 2009; 8 June 2009. *Eureka Street,* 2 February 2009; 5 June 2009; 28 August 2009; 4 June 2010. *Fire Australia,* June 2009. *History Australia,* Vol. 6, No. 2, 2009. *InPsych,* June 2009. *The Lamp,* March 2009. *The Monthly,* March 2009; July 2009. *National Emergency Response,* Autumn 2010. *Police Journal,* June 2009. *Psychotherapy in Australia,* August 2009. *Quadrant,* July–August 2009. *Sunday Telegraph,* 8, 15 February 2009; 1 August 2010. *Sun-Herald,* 1 August 2010. *Victorian Police Association Journal,* August 2009. *Water,* February 2010

Australian Defence Force, 'Black Saturday: An Articled Clerk's Relief Mission', May 2009

Victorian Bushfires Royal Commission, Final Report – Summary, 2009; Final Report – Summary, 2010

YouTube's favourite koala

21 Shipwreck at Christmas Island

AAP National News, 19 December 2010. ABC News Online, 20 December 2010. *Age*, 17 December 2010; 24 January 2011. *Australian*, 16 December 2010; 25 January 2011. *BBC News*, 16 December 2010. *Daily Telegraph*, 15, 16, 17 December 2010. *Herald Sun*, 16 December 2010; 24 January 2011. *The Sydney Morning Herald*, 17, 18, 20 December 2010. *WA Today*, 15 December 2010

'Christmas Island Boat Tragedy Report Out', 24 January 2011 http://news.ninemsn.com.au

Customs and Border Protection Media Release, 'Christmas Island Chronology', 16 December 2010

Networks 9, 7, 10 and ABC TV news reports

22 The Queensland Floods

Australian Women's Weekly, March 2011. *Brisbane Times*, 11 January 2011. *Daily Telegraph*, 12, 14, 15, 18, 20 January 2011. *Herald Sun*, 26 January 2011. *Sun-Herald*, 16 January 2011. *Sydney Morning Herald*, 28, 30 December 2010; 12, 14, 20, 21 January 2011. *Weekend Australian*, 15–16 January 2011

'Queensland Floods' http://www.qld.gov.au/floods/

Queensland Police Service Media Release, 'Death Toll from Queensland Floods', 24 January 2011

INDEX